58-9293 (10-18-69)

Famous Biographies for Young People

Famous
Negro Heroes of America

Books by Langston Hughes

ADULT

THE WEARY BLUES

THE DREAM KEEPER

SHAKESPEARE IN HARLEM

FIELDS OF WONDER

ONE-WAY TICKET

NOT WITHOUT LAUGHTER

THE WAYS OF WHITE FOLKS

THE BIG SEA

MONTAGE OF A DREAM DEFERRED

LAUGHING TO KEEP FROM CRYING

SIMPLE SPEAKS HIS MIND

SIMPLE TAKES A WIFE

SIMPLE STAKES A CLAIM

THE SWEET FLYPAPER OF LIFE

THE LANGSTON HUGHES READER

JUVENILE

FIRST BOOK OF NEGROES

FIRST BOOK OF JAZZ

FIRST BOOK OF RHYTHMS

FIRST BOOK OF THE WEST INDIES

FAMOUS AMERICAN NEGROES

FAMOUS NEGRO MUSIC MAKERS

FAMOUS NEGRO HEROES OF AMERICA

Famous Negro
Heroes of America

by *Langston Hughes*

ILLUSTRATED BY GERALD MC CANN

FAMOUS BIOGRAPHIES
FOR YOUNG PEOPLE

Dodd, Mead & Company

NEW YORK

The selection on pages 191–193 from *We Have Tomorrow*
by Arna Bontemps is reprinted through the courtesy
of Houghton Mifflin Company

Ninth Printing

LIBRARY OF CONGRESS CATALOG CARD NUMBER: 58-9293

PRINTED IN THE UNITED STATES OF AMERICA

BY VAIL-BALLOU PRESS, INC., BINGHAMTON, N. Y.

To
my namesake cousin,
Langston

To
my namesake cousin,
Langston

Contents

Contents

Esteban
Early 16th Century

Esteban

DISCOVERER OF ARIZONA

 ## Early 16th Century

Among the many fabulous stories concerning the New World that were circulating in Europe during the 16th Century, none had more appeal to adventurous explorers than the fascinating tales of a group of seven wonderful cities rumored to be built of gold. No white man had ever seen these cities, said to be somewhere to the north of Mexico, and inhabited entirely by richly dressed Red Men. These fabled Seven Cities of Cibola beyond the rim of the northern desert, were declared to be rich in treasure, but no one knew exactly where to find them. The hardy Spaniards then penetrating American shores certainly hoped to find them for, by the time Cortez had conquered Mexico, the existence of these cities had come to be accepted as gospel truth. Among the Aztecs in Mexico the Spaniards had unearthed an amazing civilization, but they found no cities built of gold. These rich centers remained undiscovered, although various expeditions had set out in search of them. In 1539 another such expedition left Mexico City, headed by a Franciscan monk, Fray Marcos de Niza. It included in its party a Negro called Esteban.

Esteban, whose nickname, Estebanico, meant Little Stephen, was from Morocco where mixtures of African and Arab

13

blood had produced a population ranging in color from ivory white to ebony black. The bearded Esteban must have been very dark because, in the records that have come down to us, he is described as *negro*, and in Spanish the word *negro* means black. Esteban was an amazing man who had traveled all across the North American continent from what is now the coast of Florida to the west coast of Mexico. In his travels, he had learned to speak a number of Indian languages. This knowledge made him invaluable as a translator and guide for the Spaniards. Besides, Esteban, over a time span of more than eight years in his pathless journey from the Atlantic to the Pacific, had lived for long periods among the Indians, so he was not afraid of them, nor were the Indians afraid of him. He thus became a valuable addition to any group of European explorers strange to American shores.

In both Spain and Portugal in the 15th and 16th centuries, Negroes were not uncommon. Some had crossed the Mediterranean from Africa as seamen, others had been brought to Europe in bondage. Esteban was by no means the first Negro to come to the New World. Pedro Alonso Niño, one of the pilots with Columbus on his first crossing, is recorded as a man of color. In the years that followed, Negroes frequently were found among the crews of sailing vessels navigating the Atlantic, and the early logs of the Conquistadores record the names of a number who made the long crossing to the shores of North or South America. In 1513 some thirty Negroes helped Balboa chop his way through the tropical jungles of the Isthmus to discover the Pacific Ocean. That same year with Ponce de Leon in his search for the Fountain of Youth in Florida, there were black men. Others accompanied Menéndez at the founding of St. Augustine in 1565. When Hernando Cortez invaded Mexico in 1519, one of the

Negroes in his army of 700 found in his ration of rice one day some grains of wheat. These he planted, and so is credited with introducing the first wheat onto the mainland of the New World. And by 1523 there were so many Negroes in Mexico that it was decided to limit their entrance, since it was thought they might try to seize the ruling powers from the Spaniards—as indeed some in 1537 were accused of plotting to do, and were killed.

But the Spaniards often used Negroes to help them in subduing native peoples. Some two hundred men of color aided Alvarado to conquer the Indians of Central and South America. And black soldiers of fortune in Peru carried the body of Pizarro, the founder of the city of Lima, into the Cathedral there after he was killed in 1541. A Negro priest was officiating at Quivira in 1540, and at Guamanga in 1542 a considerable number of colored members participated in the Brotherhood of the True Cross. Black men accompanied the Jesuit missionaries to the Americas, and many of them had settled with the French in the Mississippi Valley in the 17th century. Some forged ahead to California, and among the forty-four settlers who in 1781 established the town of Los Angeles, there were 26 Negroes. But, perhaps because of the written records kept by Cabeza de Vaca and Marcos de Niza, the name of, and an account of the exploits of Esteban have been handed down in more detail than those of other early Negro explorers.

Written history confirms that more than four hundred years ago now, as a part of the ill-fated expedition of Pánfilo de Narváez sponsored by King Charles the Fifth, Esteban set sail from Spain in 1527 with some six hundred other men seeking their fortunes in that New World which Columbus had discovered. Five Franciscan monks were among the sailors, and by royal warrant, Álvar Núñez Cabeza de Vaca—whose name, Cabeza de Vaca, meant Cow's Head—was treasurer of the expedition whose fleet consisted of five caravels with billowing sails on tall masts. It was a long journey then across the Western Ocean, and when the galleons eventually reached the shores of Santo Domingo, the men lingered there for more than a month, savoring the fruits of the West Indies and refreshing themselves with the waters of the mountain springs. Meanwhile, they provisioned the ships for the onward voyage to the mainland, leaving behind a number of deserters who found this first lush island to their liking.

In Cuba a great tropical hurricane destroyed some of the ships and blew completely away some sixty men and many horses. There Cabeza de Vaca took over command of the remains of the fleet, and in the Spring of 1528 set sail for Florida, coming up the western coast to the point where the peninsula curves around the gulf. Here unfriendly Indians greeted them with war cries rather than open arms. Pitched battles developed. The heat was terrific, mosquitoes and sand flies bothersome, and fevers and other illnesses broke out. In less than three months in Florida more than half of the white men died from sickness, or at the hands of the Indians. Since they found only a hostile welcome along the sandy beaches where they had landed, and no riches, they decided to go further. But, as they sailed along the coast, a storm came up. The crafts of the Spaniards were blown on the reefs and were quickly battered to pieces by the high seas. Narváez, leader of the expedition, drowned. Only four men managed to swim ashore. Among these four was Estebanico. The other three were Spaniards, including Cabeza de Vaca.

Possibly because of the hostile Indians, the four survivors did not tarry on the coast. They headed inland through the

16

Florida palmettos, living on game, wild oranges and the food that more friendly Indians to the North gave them. Since, with no boats, they could not escape from the mainland, they decided to explore it—to follow the setting sun and see what lay beyond the horizon. Estebanico and his three companions were true adventurers, facing they knew not what unseen dangers, but curious to travel ever forward, wondering what they would see. At times they were held captive by Indians and made to serve as slaves until able to escape. It took them eight years to cross on foot, along the Gulf Coast and over part of what is now Texas, into Mexico and southward as far as the great city at its center where a Spanish Viceroy held sway. There they were again among numerous Europeans who, under Cortez, in the name of Spain had lately conquered the Indian peoples of Mexico.

In Mexico City, Esteban served under the Viceroy of Spain and at the capital he remained for three years. But, having no liking for a sedentary life, in 1539 he agreed to become one of the members under Fray Marcos de Niza of the newly organized party which intended to explore the lands to the North where, maybe, the seven storied cities of Cibola might be located, and vast fortunes of silver, gold, emeralds and turquoise were to be hoped for as a reward for discovery. With such visions of riches and fame in mind, with government supplies and Indian guides, over the mountains and through the Sonora Valley they set out toward the deserts of the North. Under the blistering summer sun, the Spaniards in the party eventually gave out. The trek over seemingly endless sands, with only parched plains ahead as far as the eye could see, became enough to discourage even the most stouthearted—and there had been no gold, no treasure, no fabulous cities anywhere along the way. But there *might be*

—just over the land's rim.

"Estebanico, you go ahead and see," said Brother Marcos. The others agreed. The Spaniards prevailed upon the seemingly tireless Negro to forge forward with a group of Indian guides to see what lay across the barren wilderness. Esteban set out on foot toward the North until he reached the San Pedro River which he followed as it ran toward the Gila. Since communication between the Spaniards and the Indians was limited, Esteban had worked out with Fray Marcos a simple system by which he might send messages back to the encampment as to what he had discovered. If Esteban discovered nothing of value, he would send back by an Indian runner each day a very tiny cross—about the size of a hand— made of two twigs. If things looked promising, he would send a larger one—a sturdy branch crossed and tied with thongs to a larger branch. If he made a really important discovery, he would send to the Spanish encampment a very big cross made from the trunks of saplings. Then they would know Esteban had come across gold, treasure, or large settlements of rich interest. With this understanding, the Negro departed.

The sun was blazing, the pathless plains and sandy desert were hot underfoot. There were rattlesnakes and scorpions, coyotes, prairie dogs that barked, buzzards that circled over-head and mountain lions that howled at night. The Indian runners wondered where Esteban wanted to go as he urged them on and on into a seeming nowhere. Of the Seven Cities of Cibola, the Indians themselves knew nothing, and certainly they had no idea where to look for them. The first crosses that Esteban sent back to the Spaniards were very small crosses indeed, no larger than the palm of a hand. But, after a number of days, what seemed at first like distant mesas rising from the desert turned out to be in reality houses—a whole pueblo of houses. The strangers distinguished, as they drew near, that some of the houses towered as high as four stories and were beautiful to behold.

Esteban had come into the land of the Zuñis, a tribe of Pueblo Indians of advanced civilization, who lived not in tepees, but in well-constructed buildings of adobe or of stone. And, though their houses were not built of gold, above many doorways were embedded turquoise and other semi-precious jewels. The Zuñis ate from gracefully designed pottery, slept on brightly woven blankets, and lived in a manner that denoted comfort and well-being. That day, from a stout sapling Esteban cut a pair of sturdy poles, made them into a cross as tall as a man, and sent a band of Indian runners bearing this cross as his signal to the Spaniards that he had made a discovery of great importance.

As soon as the Indians panted into the distant camp with the cross, the Spaniards prepared to follow them northward to see what manner of riches Esteban had found. Their hopeful crossing of what is now the southeastern part of Arizona, did not carry them as far as the Zuñi villages and they never saw Esteban again. Three battle-scarred and frightened Indians met them somewhere in the desert with the news that Esteban was dead and that they themselves were the only survivors of the Zuñi arrows that had massacred their companions. Suspicious of his mission, the Zuñi chiefs had ordered their warriors to set upon Esteban and all his band outside the walls of Hawaikuk. And it was there that an arrow pierced him through, and his body was cut into pieces as a lesson to other intruders.

Wishing at least to see these beautiful Indian cities, Fray Marcos approached as near to them as his fear permitted. From a mountain summit he looked down at their gleaming adobe houses in the distance and termed the countryside that he saw "the greatest and the best that has hitherto been discovered." Then he went back to Mexico to spread the news to others in the name of the King of Spain. Soon a host of European explorers surged into the West. Larger and better armed expeditions penetrated the lands of the Zuñi and eventually the invaders built there settlements, religious missions, trading posts, and military presidios to protect their interests. But for the initial penetration of the Europeans into this new land of gold and copper, sunshine and flowers—what is now Arizona—the intrepid Negro, Esteban, is credited with opening the way.

Crispus Attucks
About 1723-1778

Crispus Attucks

MARTYR FOR AMERICAN INDEPENDENCE

 About 1723-1778

Before the American Independence, when the Thirteen Colonies were ruled by Great Britain, governors and tax collectors were sent out from England to siphon off their wealth for the sake of the Mother Country. However, three thousand miles of ocean between the New World and the Old made it difficult for the British always to control such distant possessions with a strong hand. And as the colonial population multiplied and the sturdy New Englanders began to feel quite self-sustaining through agriculture, seafaring and small industries, their aspirations toward independence grew. But the more the colonists wanted freedom, the harsher became the restrictions which the British put upon them, and the more taxes they wished to collect from their American subjects. Customs collectors were granted broad search warrants permitting them to enter anybody's house or shop to look for smuggled goods, and the use of these warrants was often abused. Good citizens were harassed on the slightest pretext and their privacy invaded. The colonists were not free to conduct their own foreign trade. And under the English Navigation Laws most colonial products could be sold only to Great Britain, and they had to be shipped in English boats.

Then in 1765 a form of taxation called the Stamp Act was passed in London. This act was designed to place on the colonists the burden of support for the upkeep of British troops quartered among them. It was also required that they furnish lodgings for English soldiers when barracks were not available. But the indignant colonists declared that, in their opinion, no taxes should be imposed upon them except by their own consent, and many merchants refused to sell taxable goods in their stores. Soon angry boycotts and protests beset the British, and women refused to wear dresses made of English goods, making instead their own homespun cloth. Nevertheless, in 1767 England imposed a series of new taxes on colonial imports. These included tea—which they felt the people could not get along without. When riots took place because of the new taxes, the British gunboat *Romney* mounted with fifty-four guns was dispatched to Boston Harbor. Also two additional regiments of soldiers were landed on Massachusetts soil and cannon were set up in King Street, Boston, pointing toward the Town House. It was then that Samuel Adams, a distinguished leader, immediately declared that this quartering of troops in the colonies without the consent of the people was a gross violation of basic freedoms, and that these soldiers were looked upon as intruders. Meanwhile, the soldiers behaved very badly, fighting in the streets and racing horses on the Sabbath on Boston Common. Between the soldiers and the citizens ill feeling grew. Minor clashes took place and gradually tension mounted throughout New England.

Then in Boston on the night of March 5, 1770, a serious clash of citizenry and soldiers occurred. A few days before there had been various fist fights between the townspeople and the soldiers and responsible persons had complained to the Council that the only way to avoid bloodshed would be to request the removal of the troops from the city. It was widely reported that the soldiers had openly threatened to wet their bayonets in New England blood. After working hours angry crowds gathered on street corners to discuss the situation. Such a crowd had gathered in front of the British barracks on Brattle Street on the evening of March 5. In response to irritating taunts from the soldiers, the citizens replied not only with harsh words, but with very hard snowballs. Whereupon sentries tried to drive them away, striking at the people with the butt ends of their rifles or attacking them with their fists. Noses were bloodied and there might have been a battle royal had not one of the captains of the Red Coats ordered all of his men inside the barracks. But by that time, someone had rung the great bell in the Old Brick Meeting House and, taking it as some sort of alarm, hundreds of Bostonians poured into the moonlit streets and rumors of all sorts began to fly thick and fast through the night.

Near the waterfront, in the crowd milling about between Dock Square and Long Wharf, a gigantic man of color stood out above almost everyone's head. A mulatto of light complexion then in his forties, his name was Crispus Attucks. He was a seaman but lately discharged from a whaling vessel, and little is known about his life except that in his youth Attucks had been a runaway slave. Twenty years before that fateful night of moonlight and blood this advertisement had thrice appeared in the *Boston Gazette:*

Ran away from his Master, *William Brown* of Framingham, on the 30th of Sept. last, a Mulatto Fellow, about 27 Years of Age, named Crispus, 6 Feet two inches high, short curl'd hair, his Knees nearer together than common; had on a light colour'd Bearskin Coat, plain brown fustian Jacket, or brown all-Wool one, new Buckskin Breeches, blue Yarn Stocking, and a check'd

25

woolen Shirt. Whoever shall take up said Run-away, and convey him to his abovesaid Master, shall have ten pounds, old Tenor Reward, and all necessary Charges paid. And all Masters of Vessels and others are hereby caution'd against concealing or carrying off said Servant on Penalty of the Law.

Boston, October 2, 1750.

But, so far as is known, in spite of the repetitions of this ad, William Brown of Framingham never recovered his runaway slave. Crispus Attucks had taken to the high seas as a sailor. So on that night of March 5, 1770, with snow on the ground and a bright moon in the sky, he felt himself a free man allied with the citizens of Boston in their indignation that freedom to run their own affairs should be denied them by the English.

About nine o'clock that night, taunted by youngsters, a sentinel had knocked a boy down in front of the Custom House. Whereupon, other boys began to throw snowballs at the Red Coat as a crowd of men came running to the scene. Crying for help, the sentinel ran up the steps of the Custom House while someone else of his company rushed to call out the guard. A group of British privates officered by Captain Preston trotted double-quick up King Street and were met by a crowd of citizens that included the towering Crispus Attucks, and these were armed with sticks and stones. As the soldiers ran with drawn bayonets through the street, they were pelted by chunks of ice and handfuls of snow. Then the Red Coats encountered this group of men with stones and sticks in their hands. Crispus Attucks cried, "The way to get rid of these soldiers is to attack the main guard! Strike at the root! This is the nest!" And the men began to use their crude weapons against the well armed British.

Then the guns went off. An order to fire had been given. The very first shot killed Crispus Attucks. Maybe, being tall and Negro, he was the most conspicuous person in the crowd. At any rate, Attucks was the first man to lose his life in the cause of American freedom, pierced by a British bullet in the streets of Boston.

To his aid came Samuel Gray, a white man. And Gray, too, on the instant was shot dead. The next to fall was a sailor, James Caldwell. Then Patrick Carr and a boy of only seventeen, Samuel Maverick, gravely wounded, tumbled to the cobblestones. The boy died the next morning and Carr nine days later. A half dozen others were shot, but not fatally.

When the soldiers passed, there was blood on the snow. The moon looked down on an ever-growing crowd of rebellious Bostonians thronging the streets. Before midnight the entire Twenty-ninth Regiment was called out to preserve order. But by sundown the next day these same soldiers had been removed from Boston. Three thousand irate citizens in town meeting—first at Faneuil Hall and then to a larger place, Old South Meeting House—had that day demanded the removal of the British lieutenant-governor and the members of the King's Council. That afternoon two regiments of soldiers were sent to Castle William outside the confines of Boston.

This preliminary victory in the first stages of the American Revolution, said the historian, John Fiske, came about through "the sacrifice of the lives of Crispus Attucks, Samuel Gray, James Caldwell, Samuel Maverick, and Patrick Carr. . . . Their deaths effected in a moment what seventeen months of petition and discussion had failed to accomplish. Instead of the king's representatives intimidating the people of Boston, it was the people of Boston that had intimidated the king's representatives . . . and for achieving this particular result the lives of those five men were forfeit. It is, therefore, historically correct to regard them as the first martyrs to the cause of American independence."

Concerning the Boston Massacre in which they died, years later Daniel Webster said, "From that moment we may date the severance of the British Empire"—although it was not until 1775 that the War for American Independence actually began, and it was 1783 before it ended in victory. During all that time of turmoil, the citizens of Boston did not forget Crispus Attucks and the men who died with him. Each 5th of March after their death, their martyrdom was remembered by an oration in the Old South Meeting House. But when Independence came, the date for this oration was changed to the 4th of July.

The day after their deaths—while Gray and Maverick were mourned in their homes—the homeless seamen, Attucks and Caldwell, were laid in state in Faneuil Hall, and hundreds of people passed to look at these fallen heroes. Then all four men, the Negro and the whites, were buried in a single grave as thousands joined the final ceremonies.

Today there stands on Boston Common a monument to Crispus Attucks, Samuel Maverick, James Caldwell, Samuel Gray and Patrick Carr, erected by joint action of the Commonwealth of Massachusetts and the city of Boston. At the unveiling of this memorial in 1888 William H. Dupree, the Chairman of the Citizens' Committee, said, "On the 4th day of March the British troops seemed to be immovably intrenched in Boston, and the enactments of their superiors were supposed to be the paramount law of the land. On the 5th, by the death of Attucks and his comrades, submission to English law gave place to active opposition. . . . The people were masters. The real authority had been wrested from the king, and assumed by his subjects. The death of these men made the republic secure." And, long before the dedication of the monument, John Adams had declared, "On that night, the foundation of American independence was laid."

As the monument was unveiled before the large crowd gathered in Boston common, the poet, John Boyle O'Reilly read a poem entitled *Crispus Attucks*, dedicated to the "Negro Patriot—Killed in Boston, March 5, 1770," which said in part:

Honor to Crispus Attucks, who was leader and voice that day—
The first to defy, and the first to die, with Maverick, Carr and
    Gray.
Call it riot or revolution, his hand first clenched at the crown;
His feet were the first in perilous place to pull the King's flag
    down;
His breast was the first one rent apart that liberty's stream might
    flow;
For our freedom now and forever, his head was the first laid low.
Call it riot or revolution, or mob or crowd, as you may,
Such deaths have been seed of nations, such lives shall be honored
    for aye.

Jean Baptiste Pointe
Du Sable
About 1745-1818

Jean Baptiste Pointe Du Sable

FOUNDER OF CHICAGO

 About 1745-1818

ABOUT thirty years before the Declaration of Independence was signed, in St. Marc, Haiti, Jean Baptiste Pointe Du Sable was born of mixed French and Negro parentage. His father was a pirate, the mate of a sailing vessel called the *Black Sea Gull* flying the skull and crossbones from its mainmast and raiding ships throughout the Caribbean. In those days all the waters of the West Indies were plagued by pirates who often sacked and burned coastal towns, sailing away with what riches they could find and sometimes carrying off beautiful women as well. Jean Baptiste's father had stolen his wife, Suzanne, from slavery on a Danish plantation on St. Croix. He carried her off to Haiti as a prize of piracy, and in Haiti she was free.

When Jean Baptiste was about ten years old, his mother was killed in a Spanish raid on St. Marc, and their house was burned. Shortly thereafter his father took him to France and put him into a boarding school for boys not far from Paris. There little Jean made friends with another youngster from the West Indies, Jacques Clemorgan, of Martinique. Their friendship lasted a lifetime and, as young men on their return to the New World, they had many adventures together.

Perhaps for the sake of his son, the elder Pointe Du Sable decided to quit being a pirate. In Haiti where he bought land and set up a shop, he became a dealer in coffee, hard woods, and other products of the island. Soon he acquired a schooner, the *Suzanne*, named after his deceased wife. When Jean returned from school in France, he worked a few years in his father's business. Then it was thought wise that he seek his fortune in the New France of the mainland, Louisiana, a virgin field for exploitation. With his father's blessing, and in the company of his Martinique friend, Jacques, young Jean, when he was about twenty, sailed away toward the Gulf of Mexico in the little ship *Suzanne*. But he never reached Louisiana under his own sail. Off the western coast of Florida, a hurricane came up and the *Suzanne* was blown to pieces. Only with difficulty did the young men save their lives. Fortunately a Danish vessel picked them up and carried them into the port of New Orleans.

Being a Negro who had never known slavery, Jean Baptiste suddenly found himself in a city where to be colored was to be suspected on sight of being a slave. Without identification of any sort, since all his papers had been lost in the wreck of the *Suzanne*, Jean might at any time be falsely claimed by someone as an escaped slave. Fearful of this, he took refuge with a group of Jesuit monks, where he was given employment until he decided to venture further into the interior. Having in mind trading with the Indians for furs and other things which he could sell for profit, he began to make plans for travel. But first he applied for work with one of the large trading companies in New Orleans. He was turned down because of his color. This caused him to make a little boat of his own and head up the Mississippi. With his friend, Jacques and Choctaw, an Indian who knew several languages, he set out paddling his way upstream, intending to hunt and trap fur-bearing animals, and bargain for goods with the Indians along the river banks. Eventually they got as far as St. Louis, and for a time Du Sable lived with the Illinois Indians, learned to speak their tongue, to use the bow and arrow, and to hunt buffalo on the great plains. Later he went on to the shores of the Great Lakes and as far as Detroit where he worked for the British governor of the region for a time.

Jean Baptiste Pointe Du Sable was about twenty-five when a beautiful Indian girl of the Potawatomi tribe captured his fancy and he married her. Kittihawa—Fleet-of-Foot—was her name, and to marry her Du Sable had to become a member of her tribe, taking the eagle as his tribal symbol. Together they settled down near Fort Peoria where he purchased land, and soon a son was born. But the young man did not linger long at home. About a year later, in 1772, at a point of portage between the southern end of Lake Michigan and the river where many travellers passed on their way to or from Canada, Du Sable decided to build a trading post. Then an unsettled wilderness, the area was called by the Indians *Eschikagou*, or sometimes simply *Chikagou*. This new trading post prospered, and two years later in 1774 Du Sable moved his family and all the Indians of his wife's clan there from Peoria. He built for his wife a house of five rooms with a large fireplace. This house became the first permanent home, and the beginnings of the first settlement, on the site of what is now the city of Chicago. And the first child whose birth was recorded in the new settlement was Suzanne, Du Sable's daughter, whose African-Indian heritage made her a beautiful nut-brown baby, named after her Haitian grandmother, but accepted by the Potawatomis as one of their tribe. Later the Indians, in speaking of Du Sable, often said, "The first white man in Chicago was a Negro."

Through Du Sable's efforts, surrounding his trading post and home, soon a little city grew. Kittihawa's relatives and tribesmen built houses for themselves and their families and began to cultivate gardens. As a part of his business, Du Sable himself erected several new buildings: barns and poultry houses, a dairy, a bakehouse, a smokehouse, a workshop, a mill, and a forge. Traders called Du Sable's the best trading post between St. Louis and Montreal. Soon the community became a busy center and the trading post a place to house passing travellers and supply the needs of pioneer hunters, trappers, and explorers. Thus it was that this unsettled tract of land Eschikagou gradually grew into the city of Chicago—its first citizen having been Jean Baptiste Pointe Du Sable.

Described in the old chronicles as "of commanding appearance," some six feet tall, stalwart, bearded and handsome, Du Sable was a man of business acumen and intelligence as well as good-looking. To these qualities must be added that of bravery—plus curiosity—for all his life Jean Baptiste had the urge to push on to new frontiers, to explore the possibilities of lands beyond whatever might be, at the time, his own horizon. This adventuresome spirit eventually caused his arrest by the British who were then in control of the Great Lakes region. A black man who spoke both French and the Indian tongues, and who moved about freely among the Indians hostile to the British, they could not but consider an enemy. The English commander of the area who ordered Du Sable's arrest, described him as a "handsome Negro, well educated and settled at Eschikagou, but was much in the interest of the French." And at that time, after all, the British and French were enemies. Du Sable was interned at Fort Mackinac in 1778, arrested "in the name of the king." Although held in custody, he was treated kindly, and was free to hunt and fish in the woods surrounding the fort. Since there were no actual charges against the man, he was after a number of months released to return to his family.

Du Sable's relations with the Indians grew ever closer and at one time he was proposed as the chief of the tribe. His businesses prospered. His children grew up, married, and grandchildren came. In 1800, as old age approached, Du Sable sold his Chicago interests to a St. Joseph firm, the bill of sale and the amounts received being recorded in the Wayne County Building in Detroit. Eventually he settled down in semiretirement in St. Charles, Missouri, where his son, Jean Baptiste, Jr., lived. But, since through this small frontier town almost daily came groups of horsemen and strings of covered wagons heading westward, the ever venturesome Du Sable soon began to dream of the wide open territories beyond the Missouri River. His son, however, dissuaded him of further pioneering at his age. So he contented himself with exchanging stories with the frontiersmen who passed his way. He sometimes translated for them when they needed to bargain with the Indians. And he loved the masses at a nearby Catholic church, and the conversations of the priests.

In the late summer of 1818 Jean Baptiste Pointe Du Sable died and was buried in St. Charles Borromeo Cemetery among the graves of numerous other pioneers of the West. As the founder of America's second largest city, his memory is kept alive today in the archives of the Chicago Historical Society. And a beautiful book has been written about him by another Negro American—Shirley Graham's *Jean Bapiste Pointe Du Sable*.

Paul Cuffe

1759-1817

Paul Cuffe

SEAMAN AND COLONIZER

1759-1817

Paul Cuffe spent all of his life on or near the sea. When he was sixteen he signed on a whaling vessel out of New Bedford heading for the Bay of Mexico. When he was twenty he himself built a boat for coastal trading in New England waters. When he was twenty-five he bought a fishing schooner and sailed it to St. George's Banks in search of cod. At thirty-five Cuffe owned his own whaling boats. And by the time he was forty he was the captain of vessels sailing to the West Indies and across the Atlantic. Through the tropical hurricanes of the Caribbean and the lashing winter storms of the Western Ocean, Cuffe sailed his vessels and never lost a ship.

Paul was born in 1759 on the southernmost of the Elizabeth Islands, Cuttyhunk, off New Bedford, a decade and a half before George Washington gathered his armies to free New England from the British. Paul's father had been brought from Africa as a slave, but had purchased his own freedom. He married an Indian woman of the Wampanoag Tribe and, among their ten children, Paul was the youngest of the sons. When Paul was in his early teens his father died, then the boys in the family had to provide for their sisters and mother.

Young Paul became a sailor on a whaling vessel, and learned to man the mainmast and harpoon the monsters of the sea. Down around the tip of Florida into the Bay of Mexico and to the various islands of the West Indies he sailed. During the Revolutionary War he was captured by the British and held prisoner in New York for some time.

During the War seagoing became dangerous for Americans, so for a while Paul settled down on a farm near Westport, Connecticut, tilling the soil by day and studying navigation at night. By candlelight or the light of an open fireplace, he pored over charts of the seven seas and worked with compass and navigator's rules. His limited schooling made books hard for him, but he persevered.

Together with his brother, David, he built a small open boat and went into the business of coastal trading for himself. But David did not like the water, so both went back to farming again. Paul, however, soon built himself another boat and set out for the Elizabeth Islands with a store of goods to sell. Within sight of the coast, pirates seized his boat, robbed him of all his goods, and left him in the sea to swim ashore as best he could. Undeterred, Paul built a third boat, purchased cargo on credit, and sailed for Nantucket. Again he was chased by pirates and he wrecked his boat on the rocks trying to escape. But he managed to get back to the harbor of Westport, repaired the boat, and made a round trip to Nantucket. More than once he was robbed and beaten by the sea bandits infesting coastal waters. But Paul preferred the dangers of the ocean, even in a little boat, to the safety of the soil and the plow. And from some of his voyages he managed to make a small profit. This he saved and shortly he was able to purchase a covered boat, employ a deckhand, and make more extended trips up and down the coast.

By the time Paul got married at the age of twenty-five, he was the owner of a larger boat, one of eighteen tons, equipped for cod fishing off the St. Georges Banks. Several of his wife's brothers were seamen, and together they established a profitable business in the Westport River. The same year in which Paul Cuffe married, the State of Massachusetts granted to its Negro citizens all the rights of full citizenship. And this development came about largely through Cuffe. He and his brother John had petitioned the legislature for the right to vote and other civil rights, but their petition was unsuccessful. "Taxation without representation" had been the rallying cry of the Americans in the Revolutionary War against the British which had just ended. Taking this slogan to heart, free Negro Americans like the Cuffes saw no reason why this maxim should not apply to them also. Yet they were asked to pay taxes without having the right to elect representatives. Paul and John Cuffe refused to pay their taxes and a suit ensued. The attention which this attracted to the problems of free Negroes in the new Republic just after a war for freedom, so moved the liberal lawmakers of Massachusetts that they granted the ballot to the Cuffes and all other colored citizens within the Commonwealth.

Not only was Paul Cuffe a good seaman, but he was an active citizen in all the affairs of his community. When his children were small there was no school in the vicinity of his farm on the Westport River, so Cuffe proposed a community school to be built in cooperation with his neighbors. Numerous meetings were held concerning the proposal, but it finally came to naught, possibly because some of the people did not wish to go into a cooperative project with a colored man. Paul Cuffe then, with his own funds and on his own land, built a school, employed a teacher, and invited all the parents who wished to send their children there to do so without charge. Meanwhile, as seaman and boatbuilder Cuffe's activities continued to expand. With his brothers-in-law he constructed a twenty-five ton vessel and made a number of successful voyages to Belle Isle and Newfoundland. With the profits from these trips they jointly bought a ship "of 42 tons burthen" that made several more trips up the coast. Then in 1793 Cuffe went back to whaling, setting out with two boats of his own ownership on an expedition that netted seven whales, two of which he himself harpooned. This voyage was a most profitable one. At the port of Philadelphia Cuffe sold his cargo of sperm oil and whale bone for sufficient money to purchase the materials for a third ship, the keel of which he laid on his return to Westport. This schooner of upright masts and billowing sails was called the *Ranger* and was "of 69 tons burthen" when completed. Loading it with a $2,000 cargo, Cuffe headed for Norfolk.

On the return trip, Cuffe heard of a plentiful harvest of Indian corn on the Eastern Shore of Maryland, so he steered his vessel into the mouth of the Nanticoke River with the intention of purchasing a cargo. The Maryland whites were so amazed at seeing a large beautiful ship manned entirely by Negro sailors, that they did not want to allow Captain Cuffe and his men to come ashore. Indeed, they asked him to withdraw at once from the river. In a land of slavery, whites were not accustomed to associations with free Negroes, and many did not dream that any black man alive had enough money to purchase a shipload of corn, let alone claiming ownership of an ocean going vessel. Captain Cuffe was required to produce all his papers of ownership, as well as proof of his captaincy and capabilities as a navigator. Finally his papers were declared in order and he and his men were permitted ashore.

The members of the crew of the *Ranger* were all intelligent young Negroes, polite and well behaved, and so remained in Maryland several days without incident. But the whites tried to prevent them from in any way associating with their slaves, for fear the sailors would fill their heads with ideas of freedom, or incite them to revolt. From the sale of the 3,000 bushels of corn which Cuffe loaded aboard his vessel, he made sufficient profit on his return to Westport to purchase a new house and farm, the running of which he turned over to one of his brothers. Cuffe himself continued at sea, bringing back from the South, corn, molasses, gypsum, and other profitable products for resale in New England.

By the early 1800's Cuffe had become the owner of several ships, one a brig of 162 tons commanded by a nephew, Thomas Wainer, while Cuffe himself sailed the *Alpha*, a larger vessel of 268 tons. Then he acquired a half-interest in a handsome two-mast square rigger called the *Traveller* with a lower fore-and-aft sail. This sturdy vessel made a crossing from New England to Sierra Leone, West Africa, in two months under Wainer's charge, but with Cuffe aboard as financial backer. This voyage to Africa and Cuffe's subsequent interest in that continent as homeland for the Negro people, eventually caused him to become one of the important figures of his times, with the record of his activities duly inscribed in history.

Paul Cuffe had been born free. But it was not until more than a hundred years later that Abraham Lincoln signed the Emancipation Proclamation granting freedom to the majority of the Negroes in the United States. Under slavery some Negroes bought or worked out their freedom, as Cuffe's father did; others ran away into the free states or Canada and some were born of free parents. But all over the United States the position of the free Negro gradually became more and more precarious so long as slavery existed. There was danger that any free person of color might falsely be claimed as a slave and carried off into servitude, with the courts loath to interfere. Also, Southern slave owners greatly resented any large body of free blacks being at large, agitating for freedom for their brothers still in bondage, and setting a living example of the values of belonging to one's self alone, not to any master.

In the Northern communities where free Negroes were tolerated, prejudice against them often made it difficult for them to find work. In hard times, white laborers resented employment being given to blacks, and race riots ensued. Nevertheless, free Negroes continued to strive for equal rights both as workers and citizens. In some tolerant communities such as the New England coastal cities which Paul Cuffe knew, a colored man, *with great industry*, might manage to get ahead in the world as Cuffe did. But some Negroes felt that with so many pressures against them, it would be better to look for a home elsewhere than in the United States. A few turned to Canada. Others dreamed of far-away Africa, their ancestral homeland. But Cuffe, on behalf of his oppressed brothers, did more than dream. He went to Africa to investigate the possibilities of colonizing there.

Cuffe's first trip convinced him that there were interesting opportunities in Africa for the free Negroes of America, since he saw with his own eyes the riches of the Dark Continent. The English in 1787 had taken over as their colony, Sierra Leone. There on New Year's Day, 1811, the *Traveller* arrived in port, and Paul Cuffe immediately arranged for a series of conferences with the governor and other high officials relative to settling American families of color in that land.

The Friendly Society of Sierra Leone was then created for such a purpose. After a brief sojourn, Cuffe set sail for London to pursue the matter further at the seat of British power. In England he secured the goodwill of such men as the English abolitionist William Wilberforce. Meanwhile he loaded his ship with a cargo of goods for the Friendly Society and returned to Sierra Leone with British permission to transport from the United States a group of Negroes to instruct the natives in agriculture and manual arts, the immigrants in turn to be provided with land and farming implements. From Sierra Leone Cuffe returned home to Westport greatly heartened at the prospect of eventually aiding large numbers of American Negroes to migrate to West Africa.

He planned to make at least one voyage a year to Africa. But soon after Cuffe's return to New England the War of 1812 against the English began, and intercourse with Britain or British colonies was considered treasonable. Meanwhile, Cuffe travelled to most of the large cities of the East rallying free colored men to the cause of African colonization. In New York and Philadelphia two large societies were formed for this purpose. But it was not until the War was over that any further practical steps could be taken. Just before Christmas in 1815 Paul Cuffe again sailed on the *Traveller* headed for Sierra Leone. This time he transported to Africa nine families —in all thirty-eight free persons of color—himself bearing all the expenses.

This was the first effort at African colonization by Americans and, as such, it attracted wide attention. Great debates sprang up all over the country among both white and Negroes as to its value. Southern whites particularly, being slave holders, approved of Cuffe's plans, for they saw in their extension a way to get rid of all free Negroes whom they felt were a menace to the practice of slavery—as indeed they were. Soon the American Colonization Society was organized with most of its officers Southerners, and such slave holders as the Kentuckian Henry Clay and John Randolph of Virginia among its prominent members. Federal aid for the establishment of an American Negro colony in Africa was solicited, and shortly the territory of Liberia in West Africa was purchased by the government for that express purpose. At once white abolitionists and free Negroes attacked the Liberian project as one designed to deprive free colored citizens of what few rights they had in the United States, and to leave slavery triumphant everywhere. Said the free colored people of Hartford, "Why should we leave this land so dearly bought by the blood, groans and tears of our fathers? This is our home."

Most American Negroes did not want to go to Africa at all, and Cuffe's well meaning scheme also began to be bitterly attacked. In Philadelphia three thousand colored people led by Bishop Allen branded African colonization "an outrage" and refused to endorse emigration to Liberia, Sierra Leone, or any other land outside the United States. In spite of the hardships Negroes suffered, they declared their intention to remain in "the land of the free and the home of the brave" and attempt to bring to realization the Declaration that all men are endowed "with certain unalienable rights; that among these are life, liberty, and the pursuit of happiness." Such rights, they thought, should belong to Negroes, too.

Paul Cuffe made no more voyages to Africa. The youngster who had begun his travels as a whaler and ended them as an international figure in the affairs of his country (and, indirectly one of the creators of the Republic of Liberia) died on a bright September day in 1817 just before the leaves of New England began to turn the ruddy colors of autumn. To his family he left what was, for that time, a large estate. To seamen he left memories of his skill and heroism as captain and navigator of ships of sail. To Negro Americans he left a new awareness of their one-time homeland, Africa. Even if few in the United States wanted to migrate there, Paul Cuffe saw Africa as a land of great beauty, great possibilities, and a great tomorrow. He himself had been there and knew.

Cuffe was a Quaker. Over his grave behind the Westport Meeting House, the Society of Friends have dedicated a monument to his memory. The brief inscription reads:

In Memory Of
CAPTAIN PAUL CUFFE
A Self-Made Man
Patriot, Navigator, Educator,
Philanthropist, Friend
A Noble Character

Gabriel Prosser

 About 1775-1800

Gabriel Prosser

FREEDOM SEEKER

 About 1775-1800

Freedom is a mighty word—and a word best understood
perhaps by those who do not possess it. When at Jamestown,
Virginia, in 1619 a Dutch man-of-war put ashore into bondage twenty Africans, the roots of slavery were planted in our
soil. For two hundred and fifty years those roots were to
grow, gnarled and twisted and ugly, until every foot of
American soil eventually became infected by them. And,
after Emancipation, for generations in one form or another,
the evil aftermaths of slavery lingered in our national life.
Nobody ever enjoyed being anybody else's slave, so means of
escape were always being devised. In the slave ships of the
17th and 18th centuries many captive Africans died of their
own will, suicides. Some chained in groups leapt into the sea,
pulling others after them. And hardly had slavery begun on
American soil than slaves began to run away—into the woods,
into the swamps, into the sea, anywhere to be free. Some took
refuge with the Indians, many fled to Canada. Some organized
revolts and attempted to fight their way to freedom. Freedom
is a very powerful word indeed.

Slavery meant more than being forced to work without pay. Slavery meant no freedom of movement, no visit-

53

ing of friends, no travelling without permission. Slavery meant being struck or beaten at the whim of a master or a mistress. It meant seldom if ever marrying whomever one might love. It meant seeing sons and daughters sold away, families separated, friends divided. It meant no right to assemble freely, even for religious services, without special permission. It meant eating whatever was given you, sleeping in whatever shacks were provided and doing whatever one was commanded to do, no matter how hard or distasteful the tasks. In short, it meant that a slave was entirely at the will of the master. That some masters treated their slaves well, there is no question. But that many treated them badly is also clear, particularly on the great plantations managed by overseers whose job it was to get as much work from a slave as possible with as little expenditure of money needful for food or clothing. An old slave song said:

We raise de wheat,
Dey give us de corn.
We bake de bread,
Dey give us de crust.
We sift de meal,
Dey give us de huss.
We peel de meat,
Dey give us de skin.
And dat's de way
Dey take us in.

Who could possibly want to be a slave under such conditions?

Historical records and advertisements for fugitive Negroes indicate that there were thousands of runaways. The records indicate, too, that hundreds of slave revolts took place in both the North and the South in colonial days as well as after Independence. As early as 1663 in Virginia slave uprisings are reported. In New York in 1712 nine persons were killed in a rebellion. In 1741 in that same city nineteen slaves were hanged for plotting an uprising, thirteen were burned at the stake, many publicly whipped, and a large number sold in chains into the deep South. The punishments meted out by slaveholders to rebels were usually excessive, inspired both by terror and a practical determination to keep their human property in bondage at any cost. In spite of almost certain death if discovered, slaves continued to rebel right up to the end of the War Between the States in 1865. Of the great slave rebellions, four stand out in history as having attracted wide attention: that in 1739 at Stono in South Carolina in which more than seventy persons, white and black, lost their lives; that of Gabriel Prosser in 1800 near Richmond; of Denmark Vesey in 1822 at Charleston; and of Nat Turner in 1831 in the Virginia countryside. These revolts were all unsuccessful in so far as freeing the blacks involved went, but they shook the institution of slavery to its foundations.

In the year 1800 Gabriel Prosser was a dreamy-eyed young coachman of twenty-four. He was a man of few words and his dark impassive face looked as if it were carved from ebony. He belonged to Thomas Prosser of Henrico County from whom he had taken his second name. But mostly folks called him just Gabriel, and the revolt which he organized became known as "the great Gabriel conspiracy." Of all the slave uprisings in the South, some historians consider Gabriel's the most significant in its effects upon the ever tightening codes of slavery. Certainly it spread fear of the slaves in an ever-widening circle from Richmond throughout the entire white South. And there might have been a most frightful massacre in the city of Richmond had it not been that the elements intervened on the night set for slaughter.

Gabriel had planned his revolt very carefully, and he must have been a man of great persuasive powers to be able to swear so many people to secrecy in so dangerous an enterprise. But his Negro followers were said to number well over a thousand. There were in Virginia in 1800 about 347,000 slaves, of whom some 32,000 were in the city of Richmond and its surroundings. But the white population of Richmond was only about 8,000 persons. Some of these were French and some were Quakers—minorities, to be sure, but of liberal tendencies. These groups, Gabriel felt, would be sympathetic to his cause—the French because of the ideals of their Revolution, *Liberté, Egalité, Fraternité,* and the Quakers for their known opposition to slavery and all for which it stood.

As early as April Gabriel began to make active plans for a slave uprising at the time of harvest when the grain would be ripe, the gardens full, and fruit hanging from the trees. Then, he reasoned, for Negroes who would be no longer dependent on their masters, there would be plenty to eat. In his own mind he set the date of the revolt for the very end of August, and on the first of September he planned to occupy Richmond, killing all of the slave owning whites, but sparing the French, the Quakers, and poor old women who owned no slaves. Throughout the summer he met secretly with groups of his fellow slaves, never gathering twice in the same place or at the same time. Sometimes groups would meet in a smokehouse, again in a tannery, sometimes in a cabin, other times in a grove, sometimes at a crossroads late at night. Gradually Gabriel had several hundred men and women of bondage sworn to uphold him in a mighty bid for freedom for all.

Gabriel thought that if enough Negroes could be united to seize Richmond from the whites, other slaves in all the surrounding countryside would join them in taking over the houses and lands of the masters throughout Virginia. Then he would set up an empire of newly freed slaves with himself at the head. Behind those wide eyes in his impassive face there was a very great dream—*freedom for all* within the entire area with which he was acquainted. Gabriel was illiterate, but he had heard about France, and he had heard the slogans of the American Revolution. He had heard, too, of the Declaration of Independence. And if he had never heard of any of these things, Gabriel was still the kind of man who would have wanted to belong to himself, not to any other man. Even if he bore his master's name, he did not love his master.

Gabriel was a giant of a man, six-feet-two in height, and he had a friend, Jack Bowler, equally tall and powerful physically. Together with Gabriel's brother, Martin, they planned to lead a three-way invasion of Richmond between midnight and dawn on the first of September, each to conduct a group of slaves by a different route into the city. From any sharp tool available that they could find, or steal away from white tool houses, they made weapons. They cut the blades of scythes in half and made from each blade a pair of cutting irons capable of severing a man in two. They made bayonets of kitchen knives. They fashioned clubs, stole firearms, tied slingshots to forked branches. For Gabriel and his lieutenants, it was a summer of feverish activity. When they would be ready to march, every man would be armed with something, at best a gun, at worst a club or a stone. With their crude arms, they planned to take the government arsenal in Richmond.

Whenever Martin was present at a secret meeting of slaves, he expounded on the Scriptures, and quoted that part of the Bible that declared that God would strengthen a hundred to overthrow a thousand. And the assembled slaves would shout, "Amen!" for they believed that God was on their side. Meanwhile another of Gabriel's brothers, Solomon, busied himself with the making of cutlasses. Of the crude weapons of these Virginia slaves a white witness later said, "I have never seen arms so murderous." In reality they had very little with which to fight for freedom—by the end of summer only a few muskets, a peck of bullets, ten pounds of ammunition, some pikes, and twelve dozen scythe-swords. Clubs and stones did not count much. And what were fists and bare hands to subdue an arsenal? But of audacity and courage they had a very great deal.

On the last night in August, a Saturday, the slaves agreed to meet in Old Brook Swamp at a point six miles outside of Richmond, there to receive their orders from the young leader, Gabriel, and by sundown those who could get away so early had started for the appointed place from plantation and mansion, country cabin and city shop. According to an account written later by Thomas Wentworth Higginson, these were Gabriel's plans for the meeting in the swamp: "Eleven hundred men were to assemble there, and were to be divided into three columns, their officers having been designated in advance. All were to march on Richmond under cover of night. The right wing was instantly to seize upon the penitentiary building, just converted into an arsenal; while the left wing was to take possession of the powder-house. These two columns were to be armed chiefly with clubs, as their undertaking depended for success upon surprise, and was expected to prevail without hard fighting. But it was the central force armed with muskets, cutlasses, knives, and pikes, upon which the chief responsibility rested; these men were to enter the town at both ends simultaneously and begin a general carnage. . . . In a very few hours, it was thought, they would have entire control of the metropolis. . . . For the insurgents, if successful, the penitentiary held several thousand stand of arms; the powder-house was well stocked; the capitol contained the State treasury; the mills would give them bread; the control of the bridge across the James River would keep off enemies from beyond. Thus secured and provided . . . in a week it was estimated they would have fifty thousand men on their side, with which force they could easily possess themselves of other towns."

But none of this ever happened. Instead, on the Saturday night of the planned rendezvous in the swamp, "the most furious tempest ever known in Virginia burst upon the land. . . . Roads and plantations were submerged. Bridges were carried away. The fords . . . were rendered wholly impassable. The Brook Swamp, one of the most important strategic points of the insurgents, was entirely inundated, hopelessly dividing Prosser's farm from Richmond; the country Negroes could not get in, nor those from the city get out." The fields turned to bogs, the roads to rivers. From early evening on the rain came down in torrents, the wind howled and lashed the rain into stinging blades of water. In the stormy dark, pitch black and water-filled, it was impossible for the slaves even to see the roads, and short cuts across meadows or paths through forests were utterly indecipherable. Only a few hundred men were able to slosh through water or wade through mud up to their ankles to get to the appointed meeting place in the swamp. Gabriel's expected thousand dwindled to a miserable soaked group of faces that he could not even see in the dark and the rain. For any of them to reach Richmond that night would have been impossible. There was nothing for him to do but dismiss them, and before they could reassemble, they were betrayed.

The slaves who betrayed them were named Tom and Pharaoh, and they belonged to a Mr. Moseby Sheppard whom they considered a kind master. Tom and Pharaoh did not wish their master to be killed, so on the very day that Gabriel's great meeting was planned, they told Sheppard all about it. Sheppard in turn notified the authorities, and Governor James Monroe, of Revolutionary fame, late that afternoon called for a troop of United States cavalry to guard the city, appointed three military aides to conduct the defense of Richmond, and ordered cannon wheeled into place around the capitol building. Even as Gabriel's followers that evening were hurrying through the dusk toward the swamps, the city was prepared to blow them to bits should their plan be carried out.

But it was only the next day when the full scope of Gabriel's plot became known that panic swept the city and martial law was declared. The whites were aghast at the unsuspected danger that had threatened them. As the news spread the whole state of Virginia became alarmed. Plantations turned into armed camps and in all the cities military patrols were doubled. Everyone realized that had it not been for the unusually terrible storm of the night before, a great deal of blood might have been shed and many lives taken. In the white churches of Richmond that Sunday God was thanked for having spared their lives from Negro slaughter. Providence had protected Richmond by tempest, by thunder, lightning and rain. God, the whites felt, was on their side.

Quickly the authorities proceeded to take vengeance on

the helpless Negroes. From Tom and Pharaoh and other docile frightened slaves, mostly house servants, they extracted all the names they could of those implicated in Gabriel's plans. Some slaves were hanged without trial no sooner than they were caught. But to expose in full "the conspiracy" the governor ordered a series of trials for the hundreds of suspected slaves who were rounded up. For Gabriel himself, who had escaped, a reward of $300 was posted. Jack Bowler surrendered. Other leaders were captured. But nobody would tell where Gabriel had gone. And the soldiers could not find him in the bog of Old Brook Swamp.

When the trials began in Richmond, Higginson writes that, "Men were convicted on one day, and hanged on the next—five, six, ten, fifteen at a time, almost without evidence." So many slaves were put to death until various masters began to complain at the loss of so much expensive property. Able plantation hands and good servants were not always easy to come by, even through purchase; and among the followers of Gabriel had been some of the most intelligent and hard working slaves of the region. Finally the courts were urged to give fewer death sentences, lest they decimate the best of the slave population of Henrico County. In mid-October, as the excitement began to die down, the New York *Commercial Advertiser* reported from Richmond, "The trials of the Negroes concerned in the late insurrection are suspended until the opinions of the Legislature can be had on the subject. This measure is said to be owing to the immense numbers who are interested in the plot, whose death, should they all be found guilty and be executed, will nearly produce the annihilation of the blacks in this part of the country." Jail sentences, chains, public whippings and other punishments were meted out to many. Innocent and guilty alike suffered, for slaves had to be taught the lesson that freedom was not meant for black men and women, only for whites. But the two slaves who betrayed Gabriel—Pharaoh and Tom—were quickly pardoned for their loyalty to their master.

As to Gabriel, he too was eventually captured. They found him in the hold of the schooner *Mary* when it docked at Norfolk after a trip from Richmond. They brought him back to Richmond in chains. And so important did they consider this prisoner that the governor himself interrogated him. But Monroe reported that Gabriel "seemed to have made up his mind to die, and to have resolved to say but little on the subject of the conspiracy." It had been Gabriel's plan to make a flag for his army of freedom and to inscribe on this flag Patrick Henry's famous slogan, "Liberty or Death." But Gabriel never had a chance to make the flag. However, he must have remembered, as he sat on trial in Richmond, what would have been emblazoned on his flag had the rebellion succeeded and the slaves taken Richmond.

Except for the informers—and there were only three whose names are remembered, Sheppard's two slaves and another called Ben Woolfolk—little information could be gotten from the men brought to trial. Indeed, some refused to talk at all in court. Their very silence frightened the slave masters, astonished the prosecutors, and shook the composure of the judges. Said one slave calmly when ordered to testify, "I have nothing more to offer than what General Washington would have had to offer, had he been taken by the British officers and put to trial by them. I have ventured my life in endeavoring to obtain the liberty of my countrymen, and am a willing sacrifice to their cause; and I beg, as a favor, that I may be immediately led to execution. I know that you have pre-determined to shed my blood. Why then all this mockery of a trial?"

Gabriel's process took more time than any of the others, but from him, so newspaper accounts of the time indicate, the court learned almost nothing. The Norfolk *Epitome* reported, "The behavior of Gabriel under his misfortunes was such as might be expected from a mind capable of forming the daring project which he had conceived." Another account declared, "When he was apprehended, he manifested the greatest marks of firmness and confidence, showing not the least disposition to equivocate, or screen himself from justice." The *United States Gazette* added that the man displayed "the utmost composure, and with the true spirit of heroism seems ready to resign his high office, and even his life." Gabriel went to his death without naming anyone implicated in his plans. On October 7, 1800, he was hanged. In the wind that blew about his gallows that day, those living who were still slaves must have heard the whisper of a word—*freedom . . . freedom . . . freedom.*

James P. Beckwourth

 About 1798-about 1865

James P. Beckwourth

FRONTIERSMAN

 About 1798-about 1865

Around the time that James Beckwourth was born in Virginia, the first Yankee clipper sailed around the Horn to California. From New England in 1776 this American merchantman rounded the tip of South America into the rolling Pacific and with billowing sails continued up the coasts of two continents into the Bay of Monterey. California was at that time governed by Mexico, so Monterey was largely a Spanish speaking city. But this ship returned to New England with such tales of California riches that, from then on in ever increasing numbers, Easterners began to head West. "Westward, ho!" was their cry. The West was a land where young men might make their fortunes, adventurers find adventure, women find husbands, and pioneers discover new wealth. In spite of the length of the trips, some sea captains made enormous fortunes in the Pacific trade. But by sea the voyage west was long and expensive. Many migrants could not afford it, so they took the overland routes, and the going was rough. Nevertheless, by 1826 many fur trappers were heading overland to California, and a few years later a regular trade route was opened through Sante Fe. By the early 1840's the federal government was sending official expeditions to the West

Coast while American merchants and dealers in raw furs had become well established in most of California's Mexican-owned communities.

The northern routes across country led through high and windy passes and over snow covered mountains. The southern routes lay across parching deserts, waterless and sunbaked. Either way hostile Indians threatened the guiding horsemen and the covered wagon trains of the pioneers as they sought their way through uncharted territory toward the Pacific. In 1841 John Bidwell's party, starting out from Missouri, was almost driven crazy by the heat and thirst of the desert. When they reached the mountains, weak, and with supplies almost exhausted, they nearly died of hunger. A few years later, when winter came surprisingly early that year, the Donner pioneers were caught by swirling snows in the mountains. Unable to forge ahead in the zero weather, in quickly built huts, with food exhausted, many of them died. After the flesh of their horses and oxen had been eaten, the survivors made soup from the hide of these animals and from their bones.

In 1848 the Gold Rush began. When John W. Sutter found in the stream that propelled his saw mill, something that glittered—and that was gold—from all over the land excited thousands of men and women began the long trek to California, leaving jobs, homes, families, everything in a pioneer search for wealth.

> Oh, Susanna,
> Don't you cry for me!
> I'm goin' to Californy
> With my banjo on my knee.

Across dusty plains and over rocky mountain trails went the wagon trains, often inadequately supplied and without guides. Eventually the skeletons of many a man and horse lined the way, and new graves from the Missouri to the Coast indicated that only the hardiest of travellers had managed to go on. By sailing ship from New York to the Coast was a trip of usually more than six months. Every old unseaworthy boat that could be secured was pressed into service. Many sank before they reached the Pacific, and the voyagers were never heard of again. Yet the wave of Westward migration continued. In 1850 California had only 92,000 inhabitants. Ten years later there were 380,000. And among those who reached the Coast in that decade was the Negro pioneer, James Beckwourth.

Beckwourth's father had been an officer in the Revolutionary War. He moved Westward when Jim was a child and settled his family on a farm near a point where the Missouri River flows into the Mississippi. With his numerous offspring and even more numerous slaves, for little Jim's father was a white man and his mother a slave, a whole community was created known as Beckwourth Settlement. Although a son of his master's, young Beckwourth was officially a slave. So, at the age of about twelve, he was apprenticed by his father to a blacksmith in St. Louis under whom he worked for several years. But as Jim grew older and began to court girls, attend dances, and stay out all night, trouble brewed. The result was that he often showed up at the blacksmith's forge after dawn, late for work. Frequent reprimands did no good. One morning after a severe scolding by the blacksmith, a quarrel broke out around the glowing forge between the young man and the old, and angry words split the air. Young Beckwourth was stubborn and impudent. In anger, the blacksmith picked up a hammer and threw it at Jim, but missed. Jim in turn grabbed the hammer and threw it at his boss. Then the two men fought it out with fists, and the young man won. But he was sent packing from the blacksmith shop, his apprenticeship cancelled.

The older man, however, followed the boy to his lodgings, had him put into the street, and gave orders that he should no longer be housed or fed at his expense. In the street a second fight broke out, and the constables were called. Jim fled into hiding. That night he got onto a boat, and went down the river to seek work in the mines. Shortly he became a hunter in the southern Illinois area, supplying wild game as meat to the workers in the mines. At this he did well. Soon he had saved some money with which he took a trip by boat to New Orleans—just for fun. But Jim did not like that city. Perhaps being colored had something to do with it, for in New Orleans there was a great deal of segregation, and so a Negro could not enjoy himself in as lively a fashion as could a white man. Young Jim began to dream of going West, to the far West, as far as the Rockies. Beckwourth attached himself to an expedition of the Rocky Mountain Fur Company in charge of General Henry Ashley, heading by horse and mule train westward from St. Louis. His duties ranged from shoeing horses to Indian fighting, trapping beavers and skinning furs to hunting game for food. Provisioning of the expedition was a most important operation. Years later he dictated in his memoirs, "No company could possibly carry provisions sufficient to last beyond the most remote white settlements. Our food, therefore, consisted of deer, wild turkeys, bear meat, and even, in times of scarcity, dead horses." Sometimes an enormous buffalo provided a campfire feast for the men. At other times they might have to eat the stringy unpalatable meat of a coyote, or depend on tiny prairie dogs for a meal. Fortunately, Beckwourth's months of experience as a hunter for the Illinois mining camps stood him in good stead. He was a crack shot, and wasted few bullets aimlessly.

He was also, by his own admission, good at horse stealing. Travelling fur expeditions were always in need of horses, particularly since the Indians were good at horse stealing, too, and frequently raided white men's encampments. Horses were the cause of many skirmishes with the Indians who cared little for furs, since they were plentiful, but they loved horses. Since Beckwourth had picked up a smattering of various Indian languages, he could sometimes bargain with an Indian for a horse. If he could not bargain, he could threaten with a loaded rifle. Or he could lasso and steal a mount in a pinch, riding swiftly away, perhaps with an arrow whistling toward him. In his memoirs, Beckwourth recounts some pretty tall tales. But serious historians believe that there is a basis of truth in most of his stories. Certainly he did turn up in many places throughout the Wild West, and he did pass a long and active life as frontiersman. Physical danger became a part of daily living and unknown hazards in mapless places gave zest to his keen spirit of adventure. Beckwourth loved the rugged life he lived and, after a half century of intensive pioneering years, he was still alive to tell about it in *The Life and Adventures of James P. Beckwourth*, transcribed by T. D. Bonner in San Francisco in 1854 and published two years later by Harper & Brothers.

Beckwourth in his book did not mention his Negro heritage. Being a mulatto, he was light in complexion, and on the frontier color did not matter much anyway. There a man was a man, and that was that. Frontiersmen had to be rough and ready fighters, quick on the draw, and able to defend themselves not only against Indians, but against each other. The men who went West in those days were not milksops. They were the toughest and most rugged of characters, and self reliance was a basic quality. If hungry, they would take food. If horseless, they would steal horses. If challenged, they would fight back. Good men were so mixed up with bad men, that there was often adequate cause for even a pacifist to fight, if for no other reason than self-protection. The historian, Charles A. Beard, reports that in the rough and tumble years following the Gold Rush there was in Los Angeles an average of a murder a day. And the city was full of horse thieves, gamblers, and rogues.

From the date of his first decisive fight with the blacksmith to whom he was apprenticed as a youth, Jim Beckwourth appears always to have been able to protect himself. In skirmishes with the Indians, he was so successful that—never being felled by their bows and arrows—in time he began to believe he could not be killed by an Indian. He never was. And he was no respecter of persons when it came to a fight. Once he challenged General Ashley himself, his employer, to a fight because of a name the general called him which he did not like. Even after the general apologized, Beckwourth still wanted to battle it out. But being of a cooler head, General Ashley felt that, after all their months together, they had been through too much in common to raise their hands one against the other. Indeed, on two occasions, as the general later made public, Beckwourth had saved his life—once from a charging buffalo bull, and again when the General had fallen into the current of a swirling river and was about to go under. Beckwourth, a powerful swimmer, had pulled him out. And together they had both fought the Indians. Having been associated in matters of life and death, why fight over a word?

General Ashley's expedition returned to St. Louis with a

fortune in furs, and through the streets the bearded Beckwourth himself led a grizzly bear—the unshaven man, back
from long months in the wilderness, being himself almost as
grizzly as the animal. Everyone was paid off in full, and for
days they enjoyed the gaieties of the town. But after about a
week, General Ashley called Jim Beckwourth into conference.
As one of his most trusted aides, he decided to send him on an
important mission to Bill Sublett, the captain of his trappers
in the region of the Great Salt Lake, weeks away, as travel was
in those days. Beckwourth, meanwhile, had practically gotten
himself engaged to be married in St. Louis. But he decided to
postpone that event until his return. The urge to travel over-
came the call of love. Off he went again into the wilderness
that lay beyond the plains. With a companion, on horseback
both, and a pack mule, Beckwourth headed once more toward
the West. It was fourteen years before he returned to resume
his romance with the girl in St. Louis. And every one of those
fourteen years had their share of danger and adventure—for
they were spent almost entirely in the wilds among Indians
and frontiersmen.

When after months of travel, Beckwourth finally reached
Bill Sublett, Ashley's western agent, Sublett proposed to him
another mission—to help establish a trading post among the
Blackfeet Indians. He warned that whoever undertook this
task might be scalped, but Beckwourth was willing to try it.
In appearance, being light brown, he himself looked like an
Indian, so he could move among them without attracting too
much attention. In fact, until he opened his mouth to speak,
the Indians often took him for a tribal member. At any rate,
Jim's stay with the Blackfeet was so successful that he married
an Indian woman. Indeed, he says he married two, first one
sister, then the other, but this may be exaggeration. At any

rate, with the Blackfeet, he lived as they lived, ate what they ate, and danced their tribal dances.

Later, for a time, among the Crow Indians, Beckwourth passed as a Crow, causing them to believe that as a child he had been captured in battle by the Cheyennes, and so had forgotten the Crow language. So convincingly did this fiction work, that an old Crow woman actually claimed him as a long missing son. Suddenly he found himself part of a family he never knew he had, consisting of father, mother, four daughters, and several boys. And in honor of this lost son found, his "father" went in search of the finest young women of the tribe he could find that Beckwourth might choose from among them a wife. The bride he chose was called Still Water. But, while she remained at home, her new husband went off with the other braves to fight the neighboring tribes. He fought so well that eventually he was raised, so he says, to the rank of chief and given the proud name of Bull's Robe. As a warrior, Jim could scalp with the best of them. On his return from battle he would, as did the other Indians, paint his wife's face with beautiful colors. But one day he decided to go back to St. Louis—after almost fifteen years had gone by. When he got there, he found that the girl he left behind him had become tired of waiting for his return. She was married to another man.

For a time Beckwourth worked as a guide to wagon trains crossing the mountains to California. From coast to coast he wandered in one activity or another, Florida to Mexico, Louisiana to the Rockies. Hunter, trapper, guide, interpreter among the Indians, advisor to travellers, fur trader, go-between in the problems of whites and Indians, as a man of many abilities, James Beckwourth took advantage of almost all the opportunities his pioneer age offered—except the advantage of staying in one place and getting rich. This he never did, prefering to leave the acquisition of wealth to less restless and less adventurous men. Time after time Jim came to the big cities, and time after time he left them for the plains, the mountains and the wide open prairies—those trailess spaces of Red Men and buffaloes, vast skies and beckoning horizons.

Finally, Beckwourth bought a ranch in the Feather River Valley. But when the Gold Rush came, he headed for California. There it seems he became involved in a ring of horse thieves, so he had to get away from possible prosecution. In Denver he operated a general store and found a new wife, this being about his fifth marriage. But running a shop was too tame an existence for him. At the request of the government, he undertook a mission to his old friends, the Crow Indians, whose liking for the warpath disturbed the federal authorities. Washington seemed to feel that Jim Beckwourth might be able to show them the beauties of peace. He was well received by the Crows, but his visit had little effect on their war-like proclivities. Already in his sixties, perhaps by then Beckwourth's powers of persuasion were weak. Indeed, he himself must have been pretty well worn down by this time. The year was about 1865 when, shortly after a great outdoor feast which the Crows tendered him, Jim Beckwourth fell ill at Absaroka, and there among the Indians he died. His contribution, that of a great pioneer in the opening of the West, is now a part of history.

Frederick Douglass

About 1817-1895

Frederick Douglass

ABOLITIONIST

About 1817-1895

THE state of <u>Maryland is divided by the Chesapeake Bay</u> <u>into two parts</u> known as the <u>Western Shore</u> and the <u>Eastern</u> <u>Shore</u>. Frederick Douglass <u>was born on</u> the Eastern Shore on <u>a remote plantation</u> near the Choptank River, <u>where he lived</u> <u>with his grandmother.</u> His mother was a slave, Harriet Bailey, and as a child Frederick went by the name of Bailey, too. His father was an unknown white man whom he never saw. Frederick knew only that he had a master who worked for Colonel Lloyd, and that his master would someday take him away from his grandmother and put him to work as soon as he was big enough. Frederick scarcely knew his mother for she had been hired out as a field hand twelve miles away from her home plantation. To see her child, Harriet Bailey had to walk that distance after sundown, then be back in the fields again by morning. <u>Slavery had no regard for the love of mothers and</u> <u>children.</u> They were often separated early, or sold away from each other entirely. Little Frederick was fortunate if he saw his mother a few times during the year. <u>When he was eight</u> <u>years old, she died.</u>

By that time Frederick had been taken from his grandmother and sent to live miles away with a group of other slave children in a cabin presided over by a mean old hag named Aunt Katy who did not like youngsters and treated them very badly. Starvation was one of her forms of punishment. Little Fred was often so hungry, he recalled later, that he would "dispute with old Hep, the dog, for the crumbs which fell from the kitchen table. "Many times," he said, "have I followed with eager step the waiting-girl when she shook the table cloth, to get the crumbs and small bones flung out for the dogs and cats. It was a great thing to have the privilege of dipping a piece of bread into the water in which meat had been boiled, and the skin taken from the rusty bacon was a positive luxury."

So fared this little slave boy who belonged to Captain Anthony, chief overseer on the great plantation of Colonel Edward Lloyd who was a rich man. Colonel Lloyd owned more than a thousand slaves, as well as a number of plantations besides the one on which he and Anthony lived. His Great House was white with large wings on three sides and a park all about, neatly tended by the slaves. Then there were barns, poultry houses, tobacco sheds, blacksmith shops, wash-houses, green-houses and arbors. "Over the way from the stable was a house built expressly for the hounds, a pack of twenty-five or thirty, the fare for which would have made glad the hearts of a dozen slaves." And there was also a private cemetery of stately tombs where the dead Lloyds rested beneath firs and weeping willows. From all this family wealth, Frederick and the black children received little. As clothing until he was a very big boy, Fred wore only a single cotton shirt to his knees. Of schooling he had none, but for Colonel Lloyd's children there was a private tutor from New England. As soon as they were old enough, the slave children were given such tasks as carrying water to the fields for the hands, or they were organized in "trash gangs" to keep the yards and quarters tidy. When they were ten or eleven years old, they began to work in the fields themselves, or about the stables. By the time slaves were in their early teens, they were considered grown and ready for any sort of labor the master might require of them.

While still a child, the cruelty and helplessness of being a slave was deeply impressed upon Frederick by the whipping which a girl who was his cousin received from a cruel, drunken overseer to whom she had been hired out on a remote farm. This man had beaten her so badly that she fled for protection to Captain Anthony, her original master and still her owner. She reached the Lloyd plantation with a severely scarred back and streaks of blood on her face from a gash in her forehead. But the girl got no protection from Captain Anthony. She was told only that she probably deserved the beating she had received, and that she must return at once to the man who had given it to her. Little Frederick did not understand how her master could be so cruel to a girl. But many years later he wrote, "I think I now understand it. This treatment was a part of the system, rather than a part of the man. To have encouraged appeals of this kind would have occasioned much loss of time and would have left the overseer powerless to enforce obedience. Nevertheless, for some cause or other the slaves, no matter how often they were repulsed by their masters, were ever disposed to regard them with less abhorrence than the overseer. Yet these masters would often go beyond their overseers in wanton cruelty. They wielded the lash without any sense of responsibility. They could cripple or kill without fear of consequences."

Little Frederick saw his master whip a young woman just outside the hut where he was sleeping. Condensed from his telling of it in his memoirs, he said, "It was early in the morning when all was still, I was awakened by the heart-rendering shrieks and piteous cries of poor Esther. Esther's wrists were firmly tied, her arms tightly drawn above her head. Her back and shoulders were perfectly bare. Behind her stood old master, cowhide in hand. Again and again he drew the hateful scourge through his hand, adjusting it with a view of dealing the most pain-giving blow his strength and skill could inflict. Each blow, vigorously laid on, brought screams from her as well as blood. But her piercing cries seemed only to increase his fury. After laying on I dare not say how many stripes, old master untied his suffering victim. When let down she could scarcely stand. From my heart, I pitied her. I was terrified, hushed, stunned, and bewildered."

No wonder Frederick, even as a child, asked himself, "Why am I a slave? Why are some people slaves and others masters? These were perplexing questions and very troublesome to my childhood. I was very early told by some one that God up in the sky had made all things, and had made black people to be slaves and white people to be masters. I could not tell how anybody could know that God made black people to be slaves. Then I found, too, that there were puzzling exceptions to this theory of slavery, in fact that all black people were not slaves, and all white people were not masters."

Little Frederick learned, too, that not all white people, even in the slave country, were cruel and unkind. One of Colonel Lloyd's daughters, Miss Lucretia, took a liking to him, gave him little errands to do, and treated him with friendliness. When she knew he was hungry, she would sometimes give him a slice of bread and butter. And once when another child struck him in the forehead with a cinder, she herself washed away the blood and put a bandage about his wound. It was Miss Lucretia who first told him that it had been arranged to send him to Baltimore as a slave boy in the household of her brother-in-law, Hugh Auld. Frederick was ordered to soak himself in the creek for days until all the plantation dirt had come off his skin, then he would be given his first pair of trousers especially for the trip to Baltimore. It was the first time in his life that he had been promised anything to which to look forward—a pair of pants. These, and the trip, excited him greatly. Frederick was being sent to little Tommy Auld as a present from Captain Anthony. The voyage to Baltimore was made on one of the boats belonging to Colonel Lloyd, carrying a cargo of sheep to market there. Frederick was a part of the cargo, too. When he was delivered to Mr. and Mrs. Auld, he was presented to a bright eyed little white boy who was told that here was his "little Freddy, who will take care of you." Thus he became this little boy's slave.

Mrs. Auld was a kindly woman who had never herself owned slaves, and she treated Frederick almost as a member of the family. His duties were not arduous—running errands and looking after Master Tommy. His mistress often read the Bible aloud to both the boys. Frederick's listening to her read kindled in him a desire to learn to read, as Tommy had already done. Finally the Negro boy became so bold as to ask Mrs. Auld if she would teach him.

In spite of the fact that it was against all law and custom in Maryland to teach a slave to read, she began to do so. But, being proud of his progress, Mrs. Auld made the mistake of telling her husband how rapidly little Fred had mastered the alphabet. Instantly he ordered his wife to discontinue her teachings. "If you teach him to read," Mr. Auld said, "he'll want to know how to write—and this accomplished, he'll be running away with himself." Being an obedient wife, Mrs. Auld gave the little slave no further lessons.

But the seed of learning had been sown, and Frederick determined to carry on alone. He learned from the little white boys with whom he and Tommy played in the streets. He learned from copying the words he saw scrawled on fences, the advertisements on store signs, the mastheads of newspapers. And then, as he tells it, "By this time my little Master Tommy had grown to be a big boy, and had written over a number of copybooks and brought them home. When my mistress left me in charge of the house I had a grand time. I got Master Tommy's copy-books and a pen and ink, and in the ample spaces between the lines I wrote other lines as nearly like his as possible. The process was a tedious one, and I ran the risk of getting a flogging for marking the highly-prized copybooks of the oldest son. In addition to these opportunities, sleeping as I did in the kitchen loft, a room seldom visited by any of the family, I contrived to get a flour-barrel up there and a chair, and upon the head of that barrel I have written, or endeavored to write, copying from the Bible and the Methodist hymn-book and other books which I had accumulated, till late at night, and when all the family were in bed and asleep."

Why, Frederick wondered, should he have to learn alone in secret while little white boys learned openly? Why should his master forbid him to be taught? He could not feel badly toward the kindly Mrs. Auld, for even then he realized, as he later wrote, "We were both victims to the same overshadowing evil, she as mistress, I as slave." It was all a part of the same pattern, the beatings on the plantations, the denials in the city, the refusal of learning. "To make a contented slave, you must make a thoughtless one. It was *slavery*, not its mere *incidents* that I hated. I had been cheated. I saw through the attempt to keep me in ignorance. I saw that slaveholders would have gladly made me believe that in making a slave of me, they were merely acting under the authority of God, and I felt to them as to robbers and deceivers." The helpless youngster dreamed of a way out. "I wished myself a beast, a bird, anything rather than a slave."

Meanwhile, he had come across a book with words in it like *freedom*. It was a book of speeches, noble speeches, called "The Columbian Orator," and in it were the orations of the great William Pitt, Sheridan on the Catholic Emancipation, and Lord Chatham's speech on the American Revolution. It was not a good book to fall into the hands of a slave because it was filled with ideas of liberty and freedom. Frederick purchased it himself with a half dollar that he had earned in his spare time shining shoes. At night in his garret he poured over "The Columbian Orator" and copied from it words he did not know. Later he would slyly ask someone what they meant. Frederick had determined to learn to read, and he did. And then, "with play-mates for my teachers, fences and pavements for my copy-books, and chalk for my pen and ink, I learned to write."

Growing now to be a big boy, he was sometimes sent to work in Master Hugh's shipyard, keeping a fire under the steam-box, and watching the tools while the carpenters went to dinner. About that time Frederick learned that he had not been given outright to the Aulds in Baltimore. He was there on loan. When his old master, Captain Anthony, died, Frederick was still considered a part of his estate. As such, he was ordered returned to the plantation on the Eastern Shore where a division was to be made of Anthony's property. Young Frederick had no way of knowing what might happen to him then, to whom he might be sold, or where his ultimate destination would be. His heart was heavy as he left Baltimore and the Aulds, who had treated him kindly compared to his former state of being in the country. Then, too, Frederick knew that Captain Anthony had a relative, Master Andrew, who drank heavily and was known for excessive cruelty toward his slaves. All slaves were frightened at the prospect of falling into the hands of an irrational, drunken owner. Frederick thought, suppose this should happen to him! Being a spendthrift, Master Andrew might run through his inheritance in no time, then sell him South into the cotton country, Georgia or Alabama, where he had heard that slaves were often worked to death in the blazing sun. When Frederick left the Aulds' house, not only did he weep, but his mistress wept, and little Tommy, too.

Fortunately, in the settling of the estate, it was decided to send Frederick back to the Aulds in Baltimore. But he remained long enough on the plantation to see what happened to most of the other slaves, including his relatives, who were scattered hither and yon as purchasers chose. For none did Captain Anthony's will provide freedom. Concerning this disregard of humanity, years later in his autobiography, Frederick wrote, "Now all the property of my old master, slaves included, was in the hands of strangers. All remained slaves, from the youngest to the oldest. If any one thing served to deepen my conviction of the infernal character of slavery and fill me with unutterable loathing of slaveholders, it was their base ingratitude to my poor old grandmother. She had served my old master faithfully from youth to old age. She had peopled his plantation with slaves; she had become a great-grandmother in his service. She had rocked him in his infancy, attended him in his childhood, served him through life, and at death closed his eyes forever. She was nevertheless a slave—a slave for life—a slave in the hands of strangers; and in their hands she saw her children, her grandchildren, and her great-grandchildren divided like so many sheep; and this without being gratified with the small privilege of a single word as to their, or her own, destiny." Thought again her teen-age grandson, Frederick, as he was sent back to Baltimore, "Oh, to be a beast, a bird—anything, anything but a slave!"

This time Frederick's stay in Baltimore was short for, with him, from the Anthony estate the Aulds had also been sent a badly crippled slave girl named Henny. Finding her of no use, they soon returned her to the plantation. This so angered the other heirs that they demanded that the Aulds also return Frederick. So he, too, was shipped back to the desolate Eastern Shore. Then about sixteen years old, Fred found himself in the service of a third master, another Auld named Thomas, in the village of St. Michaels. This man and his wife had been among the poorer relations in the family and so were not used to having slaves. To show their authority they treated them with a cold and distant sort of meanness which they thought indicated aristocracy. They also starved them. To get enough to eat, Frederick had to learn to steal. In St. Michaels he lived a miserable life indeed. His only pleasure came in being asked to conduct a Sunday School in the home of a free Negro, James Mitchell, who had a Bible and a few old spelling-books. The pupils wanted to learn to *read* the Testament as well as understand it. Of the former objective the whites of the village soon became aware—Negroes being taught to read! On the second Sunday of Frederick's class, in rushed his master, heading a mob of other irate whites armed with sticks and stones. The Sunday School was broken up and the slaves were driven away with the command never to assemble again for such a purpose. As for Frederick, he was threatened with shooting if he attempted any further teaching in St. Michaels.

Thomas Auld did not like Frederick, and the tall young slave, on his side, found it difficult to hide his contempt for his master, especially after repeatedly having witnessed the cruel lashings which Auld gave the poor crippled girl who also had become his property. Thomas Auld frequently whipped Frederick, but there was something about the stubborn silence with which the young slave received his beatings that irritated Auld no end. Frederick bore these whippings stoically, but it hurt him deeply to see this girl, a cripple, beaten. Finally the master accused Frederick of allowing his favorite horse to run away once too often. As punishment he announced that he intended to send the young slave to the farm of a man named Edward Covey, famous in the region for his ability to tame obstreperous blacks. Other slave owners often sent their Negroes there "to be broken" and after a twelve month period they were returned to their masters so cowed and docile that no more trouble was had from them ever.

Covey's farm was located on a wild and desolate point jutting out into Chesapeake Bay. Down the bleak road to this farm on New Years Day of 1834 Frederick trudged, his worldly belongings in a bundle at the end of a stick across his shoulder. His heart was heavy. Although he was glad to be leaving the hunger of his master's house, he feared the brutality of his new abode, for Covey was known to be free with the lash, the club, or any other object of punishment at hand with which to abuse a slave. Shivering in the bitter cold as he hurried along, Fred thought that now, "I am given to understand, like a wild young working animal, I am to be broken to the yoke of a bitter life-long bondage." Then he heard in his mind again the word *freedom*, and the word *liberty*—those words that ran all through "The Columbian Orator." But shortly before his eyes loomed the unpainted wooden house of the slave-breaker, Covey, and beyond that the barren sands and foam-white waters of the icy Bay. Through the scraggly pines at the road's end howled a bitter winter wind. This was no happy New Year for Fred.

After only three days with Covey, Fred was beaten so severely that he could hardly walk. He had lost control of a yoke of oxen hitched to a load of wood he had been sent to gather in the pine forest. Frederick had never driven oxen before and had had no instructions from Covey on how to manage them. The beasts ran away, smashed into the entrance of the farm with the load of wood, and broke the gate to splinters. Covey immediately ordered Frederick back to the woods, but this time without the oxen. The big white man walked behind the frightened boy. There in the woods on the freezing cold day, he ordered the boy to take off his clothes. Meanwhile he cut from a strong sapling a number of long stout branches commonly used as ox-goads. Then he looked at Frederick who had not taken off a single garment.

"If you will beat me," Fred thought, "you shall do so over my clothes." He made no move, in spite of threats and curses from Covey, to remove them. Then it happened. The enraged slave-breaker, he said, "rushed at me with something of the savage fierceness of a wolf, tore off the few clothes I had on, and proceeded to wear out on my back the heavy goads which he had cut from the gum tree. . . . This flogging was the first of a series of floggings. During the first six months that I was there I was whipped, either with sticks or cowskins, every week. Aching bones and a sore back were my constant companions. I was made to drink the bitterest dregs of slavery during the first six months of my stay with this man Covey. We worked all weathers. It was never too hot or too cold; it could never rain, blow, snow, or hail too hard for us to work in the field. I was somewhat unmanageable at first, but a few months of this discipline tamed me. Covey succeeded in breaking me—in body, soul, and spirit." Or so, in his despondency, Fred thought as spring turned into summer, the sun grew hotter, and the work in the fields became even harder.

But there was in this young Negro—in spite of what he thought—something that refused to be broken. One day in August Covey beat him almost to death, kicking him, then striking him in the head with a hickory slab as he lay half-fainting on the ground. Fred's offense had been unintentional. He had become ill from a long day in the heat of the treading-yard where wheel-horses trampled the straw from the grain. In the blazing sun, his head grew dizzy, ached violently, and his strength left him. He could not keep from sinking to the ground in the dusty yard, the world whirling, his stomach heaving, his breath short. Covey ordered Fred to rise, and when he could not, began to kick him with his heavy boots. Finally Fred staggered to his feet, only to fall again. It was then that Covey split his head with the hickory slab and left him bleeding on the ground. When Fred came to his senses, he resolved to go back to his real master and plead most humbly to be removed from Covey's farm, lest he die there. Battered and bruised as he was, he managed to steal away across the fields without being detected and walk the seven miles to St. Michael's.

Thomas Auld at first seemed moved by Fred's bloody and woe-begone appearance. But true to the slaver's code, that night he ordered the boy back to Covey's place to serve out the rest of his year. And Fred was commanded never to come to him again with such complaints. Auld did let the wretched boy spend the night in St. Michael's before returning to Covey for a second punishment as a runaway. On his way into the farm on Sunday morning, Fred passed Mr. and Mrs. Covey on their way to church. That day the slave-breaker did not molest him—for Covey did not think it right to whip slaves on the Sabbath. But the next morning when he approached Fred to beat him once more, something happened of which Covey never dreamed. The young Negro had resolved in his own mind not to allow any man to so mistreat him again.

At dawn as Fred was tending the horses in the stable, Covey sprung at him from behind and flung him to the floor, intending to tie his legs, so that he might then whip him without difficulty. But young Fred was too quick for the older man. He leapt to his feet, and each time Covey came toward him, he flung the slave-master to the ground. Fred did not wish to injure the man, but he did intend to defend himself. Covey was so taken aback by this show of defiance that he trembled in every limb.

"Are you going to resist, you scoundrel?" he shouted at the lad.

"Yes, sir," Fred replied, his hands raised to repel another attack.

Covey tried again to strike or to tackle Fred. But each time the white man came forward, the young Negro parried his blows, or flung him back when he tried to grab him. Finally in a rage Covey cried for help, and other slaves came running into the barn. But none of them, in spite of sure punishment to come, would take the slaver's side against Fred. Covey's cousin, a young man, did attempt to aid the slave-breaker, but Fred dealt this relative such a blow there in the stable that he "went off, bending over with pain," and left Covey to battle it out alone. The match spilled through the door into the barnyard where, determined not to be bested, for more than two hours Covey tried to get hold of Fred to whip him, panting and battling all the while. It was long after sunrise when he finally gave up.

"Now, you scoundrel, go to your work," Covey cried, making a pretense at having won. "I would not have whipped you half so hard if you had not resisted."

But, in reality, Covey had not whipped Frederick at all. And for the young slave, that memorable morning was a turning point in his life. "I was a changed being after that fight. I was nothing before; I *was a man* now. I had reached the point at which I was not afraid to die. . . . When a slave cannot be flogged, he is more than half free."

Probably because Covey did not want to let anyone know he had been bested by a black boy of sixteen, he never reported the incident to Frederick's master, or to the authorities. And he never attempted to whip the boy again. He tried only to work him to death.

When his term with Covey was up, Frederick was transferred on a yearly contract to a new master, a William Freeland, on a small farm near St. Michael's. Freeland was a kindly man and although Fred's work as a field hand was hard, the change was heaven compared to life at Covey's. But, kind master or not, by now Fred's hatred of slavery was so strong that he could not help but think of ways of escaping. He had heard of the North where men were not slaves, and of Canada where slavery had been abolished. Meanwhile, Fred commenced to conduct Sunday School classes again, this time in the open air under the trees during the summer. In the woods out of sight of the whites, with more spelling books than Bibles, he began to teach those who could not read. At one time he had more than forty pupils, all in danger of lashes on their backs if caught. "We might have met to drink whiskey, to wrestle, fight, and to do other unseemly things with no interruption from the saints or sinners of St. Michael's. But to meet for the purpose of improving the mind and heart, by learning to read the sacred scriptures, was a nuisance to be instantly stopped."

During his second year with Mr. Freeland, Frederick made up his mind to run away, and he persuaded five other young men in the neighborhood to make the break for freedom with him. The very thought of attempting escape made them so happy that as they worked they began to sing such spirituals as:

> *I thought I heard them say*
> *There were lions in the way—*
> *I don't expect to stay*
> *Here much longer . . .*

And another even more explicit one disguised in Biblical phrases:

> *O Canaan! Sweet Canaan!*
> *I am bound for the land of Canaan.*

Every Sunday Frederick and the five other young men met to discuss their plans—not of rebellion and the harming of their masters, but simply escaping from them and making their way North into a free state. For such plans, however, slaves could be put to death, and this they knew. On any road any white man might stop a Negro suspected of running away and hold him for arrest, or slave-catchers might seize them and sell them into the far South. Nevertheless, just before the Easter holiday they determined to start. Frederick wrote out temporary passes for each of them, such as a master might give a slave when granting permission for a visit at a distance. On the appointed morning they gathered for work in the fields as usual, "but with hearts that beat quickly and anxiously." Somehow Fred had a premonition that they had been betrayed. Sure enough they were. Shortly three constables appeared, Fred's master with them, and the six young men were quickly bound with ropes and taken into Easton for investigation. They were "drawn along the public highway— firmly bound together, tramping through dust and heat, barefooted and bareheaded—fastened to three strong horses whose riders were armed with pistols and daggers." Before the youths were taken away, the master's mother pointed a bony finger at Frederick and cried, "You devil! You yellow devil! But for you, you long-legged yellow devil, Henry and John would never have thought of running away." And it was true —Fred had put into *other* minds the thought of freedom.

Fortunately the passes Fred had forged were not found. Some of the fellows succeeded in throwing them away, others ate theirs as they were dragged panting and stumbling behind the horses fifteen miles to jail. In Easton the slave-traders crowded around them, inspecting them, and hoping to buy the husky youths for resale in the Deep South. But after several days in prison, the masters of the others came to get them, leaving Fred there alone. Finally his master came too, but trusting him no longer, Mr. Freeland sent Fred back to Baltimore where he could no longer "contaminate" his other slaves. Being a Negro with "book-learning" Fred was considered dangerous.

This narrow escape from severe punishment did not deter Fred from continuing to dream of escape. In Baltimore he was hired out to a shipyard contractor who placed him as a helper at the beck and call of all the white carpenters and caulkers in the yard. These white workers gave the young slave a hard time, a half-dozen voices at once calling him to different tasks, with threats and curses coming from every direction if he did not move fast enough to satisfy them all. And *all* of Fred's wages went to his master. Everywhere white workmen were resentful of slave labor, believing that such competition helped reduce jobs for them. This resentment they took out on helpless Negroes like Fred who were placed in the Baltimore shipyards through no will of their own. Sometimes the white workers spat at him, while vile names and curses accompanied almost all their orders. One day one of them struck Fred. When the boy attempted to defend himself, he was set upon from all sides and beaten until he could hardly stand. Finally someone dealt him a blow from behind with a hand-spike, while another worker kicked him squarely in the eye as he lay on the dock. Meanwhile, more than fifty other white shipbuilders stood around and did nothing to help the lone colored boy.

Fred's master, Hugh Auld, was outraged when the blood-covered youngster dragged himself home. Auld was angry, not so much that Fred had been injured, but that a piece of "property" belonging to him had been so badly damaged without his permission. He took Fred to the magistrate, but this representative of the law refused to arrest anyone on the mere word of a colored boy, even though his swollen face and bruised body testified as to what had happened to him. "The laws and morals of the Christian city of Baltimore afforded no protection to the sable denizens of that city," Fred later wrote as he reflected that, "Nothing was done, and probably would not have been done, had I been killed in the affray."

But Master Hugh did remove Fred from that particular shipyard. He permitted him to hire himself out, providing he turned over to his master each week all of his wages. Why, Frederick asked himself, should every cent of his hard earned money be taken from him by Master Hugh? "He did not earn it; he had no hand in earning it; why then should he have it?" So more than ever Frederick thought of again running away. One day, when he was twenty-one years old, he did. Disguised as a sailor, and with a borrowed Seaman's Certificate, Frederick boldly boarded a train in Baltimore station headed for Wilmington. He changed there to the Philadelphia boat, and that night caught a train to New York. The journey covered about twenty-four hours, without mishap. And in New York Frederick was free—at last he belonged only to himself!

Frederick got married in New York and, with his bride, he set out for New Bedford where he found work on the docks. There, as a protection against being traced, he dropped his slave name, Bailey. From a character in Scott's "The Lady of the Lake" he took a new name, Douglass—Frederick Douglass—and by the end of the next decade, that name was known all over America. Brave enough as a teenager to defy the slave-breaker, Covey; later brave enough to make an unsuccessful attempt to escape from slavery; then at twenty-one to succeed in gaining his freedom—Douglass shortly became brave enough to defy the *whole* institution of slavery by becoming one of the leading forces for abolition in the country. This took a great deal of not only moral, but physical courage. To be a *white* Abolitionist in those days was dangerous enough, reviled as they were, stoned by mobs, and even killed. But to be a *black* Abolitionist was to run greater and more frequent risks than whites ever could know. All the Abolitionists were under continual attacks by the press, accused of being in league with the devil and trying to overturn the government. Because they believed in freedom for all slaves everywhere, Douglass paid no attention to the barrage of charges against them. He thought, "Abolition—whatever else it might be—was not unfriendly to the slave." In 1841 at Nantucket, Douglass made his first speech before an Anti-Slavery Society, and from that time on he grew into one of the greatest forces against slavery in the United States.

Frederick Douglass at twenty-four was six feet tall. He had warm deep set eyes, a shaggy head of hair like a lion, a rich voice and a powerful personality. In telling his personal story of bondage and escape, he could move an audience to tears, then with logic verbally demolish the whole slave system, and cause thinking people to want to aid in its actual abolition. The unthinking, of course, would not listen to Douglass, and mobs attempted more than once to break up his meetings. In Indiana a group of pro-slavers tore down the outdoor platform on which Douglass was speaking, beat him into unconsciousness, and left him on the ground with a broken hand which never fully recovered its usefulness. Kind-hearted Quakers nursed him back to health and strength and Douglass continued his speaking tours, collecting large sums of money everywhere to aid the Abolitionists in their fight to free America of slavery.

As the eve of the War Between the States approached, and the issue of slavery more and more divided the nation, passions on both sides became ever more heated; the division grew between North and South, between political parties, and even between families and friends. Then old John Brown, a white man, began to plan his raid on Harper's Ferry in Virginia, where he intended to seize the government arsenal and free all the slaves in the surrounding area, hoping thus to start slave insurrections throughout the South. John Brown invited Frederick Douglass to join him in this enterprise. It took great courage for anyone then in any way to associate himself with John Brown, or correspond with him, or be seen in his company. Douglass did not approve of Brown's plans, thinking them impossible of fruition, but nevertheless he sheltered Brown upon occasion, and he went to confer with him at Chambersburg shortly before the eventful raid. The authorities so strongly believed that Douglass was involved in the bloody uprising at Harper's Ferry, that he had to flee to England for a time to escape unjust prosecution.

When, over the issue of slavery, the Southern states seceded and set up the Confederacy, and the War Between the States began, the Union Army would not at first recruit Negroes. Douglass urged Lincoln to do so. He reproached the North "that they fought the rebels with only one hand, when they might strike effectually with two—that they fought with their soft white hand, while they kept their black iron hand chained helpless behind them." When enlistments were opened, Douglass urged every Negro "to get an eagle on his button, a musket on his shoulder, and the star spangled banner over his head." He said, "Liberty won by white men would lose half its luster. . . . Who would be free themselves must strike the first blow. . . . I urge you to fly to arms, and smite with death the power that would bury the government and your liberty in the same hopeless grave." Among the first colored men to join the Union Army were Douglass' two sons; and thousands of other Negroes, free and slave, flocked to the colors.

At the close of the War, when freedom was won, Douglass devoted himself to the cause of complete citizenship for colored men and women under democracy. The right to vote, the right to work, the right to be treated as decently as others in public places, all these things Douglass desired for the Negro people. Not only did he speak about them and write about them, but he actively tried to achieve them. Once when a railroad conductor attempted to segregate him on a train in the North by trying to move him to a coach for colored people only, Douglass held on to the arms of his seat and refused to be ejected, even by force. Determined to make him move, several strong white bullies were called. But so tightly did Douglass grip the seat, that the seat and all had to be torn from the floor before he would be carried from the coach. Only in this way did they move this man who would not change places to please the segregationists.

All of the broad social problems of the day came within the scope of the interests of Frederick Douglass. When very few men stood up for woman's suffrage, Douglass contended that women were human beings and citizens just as men, and should therefore have the right to vote. He was associated with such famous feminists of the day as Lucretia Mott, Lydia Maria Child, and Abby Kelley. And at some votes-for-women conventions, Douglass was the only male speaker on the platform. Temperance was also one of his interests, as well as the unionization of workers, and the participation of Negroes in workers' leagues. Through his newspaper in Washington, "The National Era," Douglass often presented strongly worded views on liberal causes then opposed by most of the nation's press. A courageous crusader of the written and spoken word, Douglass so remained until his death at the age of seventy-eight.

On February 20, 1895, in Washington, Frederick Douglass had just given stirring support to the feminist cause before a large gathering. With applause still ringing in his ears, on his return home that night he paused in the hallway to tell his family what had happened at the meeting. With a gesture as if he were reacting his speech, the old man fell to his knees. For a moment those around thought this merely a dramatic way of telling the story. But when he quietly sank to the floor and did not rise again, they knew something was wrong. Frederick Douglass was dead.

In the long summations of his life that appeared the next day in newspapers all over the country, some of them repeated a story that had often been told about his very first speech—that before the Anti-Slavery Convention in Nantucket more than fifty years before when the tall young man just out of bondage stood before an audience composed largely of whites and quite simply poured out his heart to them. When Douglass had finished speaking the great abolitionist, William Lloyd Garrison, arose and cried to the crowd, "What I want to know is: Have we been listening to a thing, a piece of property, or a man?"

As one voice the audience shouted back, "*A man!*"

Harriet Tubman

 About 1823-1913

Harriet Tubman

LIBERATOR

 About 1823-1913

Some forty years before Abraham Lincoln signed the Emancipation Proclamation, Harriet Tubman was born on the Eastern Shore of Maryland, a slave, the property of the Broadas Plantation. One of eleven brothers and sisters, she was a homely child, moody and wilful as well. Harriet was not cut out at all for slavery. Very dark, and of pure African ancestry, for her grandparents had been brought from that land in chains, Harriet was said to be a descendant of the Ashanti people, among the most rebellious and warlike of Africans.

When Harriet was nine or ten years old, she was ordered into the Big House to assist the servants there. On her very first day in this capacity her mistress whipped her four times. Soon the white lady grew utterly impatient with the sulky, and seemingly stupid girl so she sent her to work in the fields. This Harriet liked better than washing pots, emptying garbage and making kitchen fires. Even a slave out under the sky could look up at the sun and sometimes listen to birds singing in the bright air. But in her early teens a cruel thing happened to Harriet, and from the slavemaster's point of view, it was her own fault.

One evening about dusk a slave boy wandered away from the corn husking to which he had been assigned and went down the road to a country store. An overseer pursued him, intending to whip him for leaving the place without permission. When he grabbed the boy in the store, the youth resisted. The white man then called upon other slaves standing about to help him. No one moved to do so. Then the boy started to run and the overseer called to Harriet who was standing in the door to stop him. Harriet did not stop him nor did she move out of the door so that the overseer could get by. This made the white man so angry that he picked up an iron weight used on the scales and threw it at Harriet. The weight struck her in the head making a deep gash and knocking her unconscious in the doorway. As she lay there bleeding, everyone thought she was dead, and she did not come to her senses again for days. Tossing and turning on a pallet on the floor of her mother's cabin, talking strange talk, Harriet's delirium caused the others in the family to conclude that she might be demented for life. Indeed, when she finally recovered, her master believed her to be half-crazy. Harriet did nothing to change his opinion—but she was not crazy. From the blow on her head there did result, though, an unusual condition. From that time on, all her life, Harriet could not prevent herself at times from unexpectedly blacking out, going suddenly sound asleep no matter where she was. Then, after a spell, just as suddenly, she would come to herself again. And the deep dent which the iron weight made in her head remained until her death.

When Harriet grew to be a young woman she determined to escape from slavery. She had never learned to read or write, she had never seen a map, and she had no idea where the North—that place of freedom—was. But, nevertheless, she made up her mind to find it. Meanwhile, she had married. She urged her husband to come North with her but he refused. She also asked some of her brothers and sisters if they would go with her but only two of them, Henry and Robert, agreed, and at the last moment, they turned back. But with company or without, Harriet had made up her mind to risk the dangerous trek to freedom.

Before dawn one morning the young slave girl gathered her necessities into a bundle and started out. For fear that her mother and others would be greatly worried upon finding her missing, perhaps even thinking that slave-catchers had kidnapped her to sell into the Deep South, Harriet wanted in some way to tell them goodbye. But to do this was dangerous, both to them and to herself. So instead, in the early evening of the night she planned to leave, Harriet walked slowly through the slave quarters singing, and she knew that all the slaves would understand her song—if not then, soon:

> *When dat old chariot comes,*
> *I's gwine to leave you.*
> *I's bound for de Promised Land.*
> *Friends, I's gwine to leave you.*
> *Farewell! Oh, farewell!*
> *I's sorry friends to leave you.*
> *Farewell! Oh, farewell!*
> *But I'll meet you in de mornin'*
> *On de other side of Jordan. . . .*
> *Farewell! Oh, farewell!*

That night Harriet stole away across the dark fields and through the woods, guided only by the North Star, heading for freedom. When she reached the Choptank River, she trudged hour after hour upstream, for by walking in water, bloodhounds trained to scent runaways, could not trail her. Eventually she found a sheltering place with kindly Quakers whom she knew to be friendly to escaping slaves. There she was rested and fed and given directions for crossing into Delaware. If the night was cloudy, she felt the trunks of trees to find on which side the moss grew, for moss indicated the northern side. Sometimes, tree by tree, Harriet headed for freedom. Sometimes she hid in caves, sometimes in graveyards, and she had many narrow escapes from the constant slave patrols that rode the highways, and from suspicious strangers who looked at the young black woman and wondered where she came from and whose slave she might be. But finally Harriet reached Philadelphia where she found work, and was no longer anybody's slave.

She said, "I looked at my hands to see if I was de same person now I was free. Dere was such a glory over everything! De sun come like gold through de trees and over de fields, and I felt like I was in heaven." But to Harriet, the North was not heaven so long as her friends and kinfolks remained in the slave country. Almost immediately she began to make plans to go back South to lead others along the hazardous road to freedom. In the years to come, it was as a liberator of slaves that Harriet Tubman became famous—a work which demanded anonimity and yet which, against her will, turned the spotlight of a nation upon her. She became one of the most successful conductors in the Underground Railroad, noted for her courage and her cunning, with at one time a reward of $40,000 offered for her capture.

The term *Underground Railroad* was applied to a widespread system of aiding escaped slaves which the Quakers and other friends of freedom had established. Eventually such friends set up way stations along several routes from South to North at which runaways could be sure of assistance. One such route ran from the coastal states of the South up to

Philadelphia, New York and Boston; another from the mid-South by way of Cincinnati to the Great Lakes and Canada. Along these routes slaves were hidden in barns, corncribs, attics, cellars, sometimes even churches. They were provided with hot food, warm clothing, perhaps a little money, and information as to where to find the next friendly family. Passwords, or the correct number of raps on a door in the night, were given; and above all from such friends came the knowledge that not all whites were out to harass and endanger those who sought escape from bondage. Sometimes when the going was rough and slave-catchers were known to be infesting the highways, workers in the underground Railroad might transport fugitives from one station to another hidden under a load of corn in a wagon with a false bottom; or a male runaway might be disguised as a coachman and put to driving a fine carriage in which a white man sat as if he were the master. When the "coachman" had gotten to a safe hiding place, the white rider would drive his carriage back home, having aided another slave to freedom.

It was dangerous, and eventually illegal, for whites to engage in such activities. But it was doubly dangerous for a Negro to do so, and especially for an escaped slave such as Harriet Tubman. But Harriet did not let fear stand in her way. Most former slaves, once having escaped, never ventured back into slave territory again. But Harriet returned to the South more than nineteen times, and each time she brought back with her to the North a band of fugitives. None were ever captured. As a conductor on the Underground Railroad she once said, "I never run my train off de track, and I never lost a passenger." It is estimated that she brought more than three hundred slaves to freedom in the decade between 1850 and 1860. First she conducted her sister and her two children North from Baltimore, then on subsequent trips she penetrated the Eastern Shore and brought out various relatives and friends brave enough to attempt the Northward journey. But it was not until 1857 that Harriet was able to get her aging parents out of the South. Since they could not walk the long miles to freedom, it took great ingenuity to transport them through slave territory by two-wheel cart. It took money, too, for train fare once they had crossed the border but eventually Harriet got them to Canada.

To earn money for her forays, Harriet worked between trips as a domestic servant or hotel maid in Pennsylvania and New Jersey. After the cruel Fugitive Slave Law was passed in 1850, which permitted escaped slaves (and even free Negroes falsely charged as slaves) to be seized in the North and sent back in chains to the South, Harriet had to accumulate enough money to buy train tickets for her fugitives all the way through the Free States to Canada. In Canada slave catchers did not operate. But from Maryland to the Canadian border was almost five hundred miles—a long journey for a man or a woman with nothing. However, as the fame of Harriet's desperate missions spread, Abolitionists of means came to her aid, funds were supplied her, food and hiding places provided, and prayer meetings held for her safety. The white abolitionists marvelled at her bravery. The New England minister, Thomas Wentworth Higginson, termed her, "the greatest heroine of the age. . . . Harriet Tubman, a black woman and a fugitive slave, who has been back eight times secretly and brought out in all sixty slaves with her, including all her own family, besides aiding many more in other ways to escape. Her tales of adventure are beyond anything in fiction and her generalship is extraordinary. . . . The slaves call her Moses."

Angered by the callous application of the Fugitive Slave

Law, and determined to help as many slaves as possible escape, the leading abolitionists of the times, white and Negro, aided Harriet Tubman in her objectives. In Wilmington, Delaware, a Quaker business man, Thomas Garrett, gave her money for train fare, food and winter coats. In Philadelphia the Negro, William Still, who kept a record of all the escaped slaves passing through his station, stood ready to help. In New York City the editors of the "National Anti-Slavery Standard," one Negro and one white, David Ruggles and Oliver Johnson, aided Harriet in pushing on to Albany with her band of runaways. Near Albany the wealthy Gerrit Smith gave counsel and funds as well as secret shelter. At Syracuse the former slave Rev. Jermain Loguen, found ways of forwarding his black brethren to the Abolitionist center of Auburn where Senator William H. Seward gave them sustenance and a place to sleep. Then at Rochester, the great Negro leader, Frederick Douglass, provided aid for the last jump to Canada. Sometimes, before a group departed on that last lap to freedom, remembering the South, they might sing:

> *Farewell, old master,*
> *Don't think hard of me.*
> *I'm on my way to Canada*
> *Where all the slaves are free.*
> *I'm now embarked for yonder shore*
> *Where a man's a man by law.*
> *The iron horse will bear me o'er*
> *To shake the lion's paw.*
> *Oh, righteous Father,*
> *Wilt thou not pity me,*
> *And aid me on to Canada*
> *Where all the slaves are free!*

One runaway, Josiah Bailey, for whom a large reward had been offered, was so frightened of being captured at the last moment that he would not even look out of the window to see Niagara Falls as the train crossed into Canada. But when Harriet Tubman and her party of eleven men and women left the coach on safe soil, Bailey then began to sing loudly and shout and no one could stop him, "Heaven! Heaven! Heaven!" Harriet, who was a plain spoken woman who did not go in for demonstrations, barked, "Well, you old fool, you! You might at least have looked at Niagara Falls on the way to heaven."

Numerous examples of Harriet Tubman's heroism have been recorded and one example is commemorated on a bronze tablet in Troy, New York. There, one day in 1869 while on her way to an anti-slavery meeting in New England, she heard that a runaway slave named Charles Nalle was that very afternoon being arraigned in Federal Court for return to slavery. Immediately Harriet sprang into action, organized a rescue party of free Negroes and whites and arranged to have a boat in readiness to take Nalle across the river to Albany as soon as he could be kidnapped from the Court. She had no difficulty in getting followers for this daring attempt for the abolitionists believed that whether a rescue attempt failed or not, it got headlines in all the papers, served to keep anti-slavery sentiment alive and was worth a hundred speeches.

By pretending to be a crippled old woman of no importance, Harriet hobbled into the courtroom to watch the process and to wait for the proper moment to give a signal to the crowd outside. When the bailiffs prepared to move the prisoner, Harriet seized the astonished slave and the crowd in the street immediately thronged about them. Harriet and Nalle made for the river but officers overtook them. A pitched battle went on for hours between officers and abolitionists that day and both Harriet and Nalle were injured in the struggle. But finally the police were bested and the boat with the fugitive started for Albany, his supporters following on a ferry. There, another battle with the authorities took place but eventually Nalle got away. That night he was safely hidden in a wagon bound for Canada. But Harriet Tubman had to go into hiding for the next day her name made headlines throughout the nation. She had taken a prisoner away from government marshalls.

Most of Harriet's rescues from slavery, however, were made without the help of crowds. They began in slave territory itself and were therefore fraught with danger. One of these dangers was betrayal. All who went North with her were, of course, sworn to secrecy but some grew weak and weary on the way. Frightened, cold and tired, they wanted to turn back. Once back on the plantation they could be beaten until they disclosed all they knew and the names of the other runaways as well as their leader. This Harriet could not permit. For weak-kneed freedom seekers she had a remedy. That remedy was a pistol which she carried in the folds of her dress. And weary ones who wanted to turn back were faced with this pistol and advised that they would either go on or be shot. They always found the strength to go on. In this way no one who started out for freedom with Harriet Tubman ever failed to become free. Her bands of runaways were never betrayed.

Because of her qualities as a leader, when the slave issue split the nation asunder and the war between the North and South broke out, Harriet Tubman went into the service of the Union Army. She became the only woman in American military history ever to plan and conduct an armed expedition against enemy forces. But before this happened Harriet served the Union cause in numerous other capacities, her basic work being as an organizer among the Southern Negroes of a branch of the government Intelligence Service at the direction of the General Staff. Newly liberated slaves in battle areas could be most useful as scouts and spies for they knew the terrain, the location of stores of food and often where rebel ammunition dumps were located. And Harriet could teach them the secret of moving quietly through enemy lines without creating suspicion. She herself often went with scouting groups and did active work as a government spy against the slaveholding forces. With this objective for her in mind, Governor Andrew of Massachusetts arranged for Harriet's transportation to South Carolina aboard the government transport, *Atlantic*. At Port Royal Harriet was given army rations but when she noticed that other Negroes, hungry and ragged and just out of slavery, grew jealous of this, she relinquished her special privileges, began to make pies and cakes to sell the soldiers and thus earn her own keep. She moved among the refugees of war—contrabands, as such liberated or escaped slaves were called in Union camps—and taught them how to keep their quarters clean, wash, sew and find ways of making a living. When epidemics broke out in the camps, Harriet served as a nurse, not only tending the sick but keeping hospital barracks clean, shooing flies and acting as friend and counselor. In fact, wherever and whenever she was needed, she would go. She became a kind of trouble shooter for the Union forces from the Carolinas to Florida.

But Harriet's most famous exploit during the war was the leading of a raid from Port Royal inland up the Combahee River. A group of her Negro scouts had prepared the way and had learned from slaves on the plantations along its banks the locations of torpedoes in the river. With a picked detach-

ment of some 150 Negro troops led by Harriet herself on a
fleet of three small gunboats and with the assistance of Colonel
James Montgomery, on the night of June 2, 1863, she started
up the river. As the Federal gunboats approached, most rebel
outposts fled, but first sent word to inland headquarters of
the presence of the Union fleet. At each plantation Harriet
ordered groups of soldiers ashore to burn houses, burn crops
that could not be salvaged for Union stores and alert slaves
to join the liberating forces. At Combahee Ferry the bridge
was destroyed and a large detachment landed to set fire to the
four rich plantations. By this time it was dawn and all the
plantations on both sides of the river had been aroused. In
vain did overseers try to keep their slaves from fleeing through
rice fields and marshes toward "Mr. Lincoln's gunboats" and
the freedom they promised. Confederate soldiers went into
action against the fleet, but with little effect. As Harriet and
her men steamed back toward the coast, all along the way they
picked up slaves who now under Federal protection, were
slaves no more. Once again Harriet Tubman functioned as
a liberator—although only incidentally now within the larger
framework of the war which would eventually free all the
slaves. Her work did much to prove how invaluable Negro
troops, and even untrained slaves, could be toward the win-
ning of that war. Eventually Harriet Tubman was credited
with freeing more than seven hundred bondsmen in the re-
gions where she and her scouts were active. Her song to them
went:

> *Of all the whole creation*
> *In the East or in the West,*
> *The glorious Yankee nation*
> *Is the greatest and the best.*
> *Come along! Come along!*

And don't you be alarmed—
Uncle Sam is rich enough
To give us all a farm.

Concerning the Combahee River raid, rebel reports blamed the inadequacy of their own command for allowing "a parcel of Negro wretches calling themselves soldiers, with a few degraded whites, to march unmolested with the incendiary torch to rob, destroy and burn a large section of the country." But the Boston *Commonwealth* reported otherwise and gave full credit to Harriet Tubman's leadership for this successful military foray. It said in part:

"Colonel Montgomery and his gallant band of 300 black soldiers under the guidance of a black woman, dashed into the enemy's country, struck a bold and effective blow, destroying millions of dollars' worth of commissary stores, cotton and lordly dwellings and striking terror into the hearts of rebeldom, brought off near 800 slaves and thousands of dollars' worth of property without losing a man or receiving a scratch. It was a glorious consummation."

Reporting the celebration which was held in Beaufort after the raid, it said:

"The Colonel was followed by a speech from the black woman who led the raid and under whose inspiration it was originated and conducted . . . Many and many times she has penetrated the enemy's lines and discovered their situation and condition and escaped without injury but not without extreme hazard."

Colonel Montgomery had already termed Harriet "a most remarkable woman and invaluable as a scout," while General Saxton said she displayed "remarkable courage, zeal and fidelity." And in his memoirs of the War, Samuel J. May declared, "She deserves to be placed first on the list of American heroines."

One of the simplest and most beautiful word pictures of a battle is Harriet Tubman's description of that at Fort Wagner at which she was present and where to Colonel Robert Gould Shaw, the Union commander, she served his last meal before he led his black troops into action and was himself killed. Of this battle, one of the Union's most bitter defeats in which more than 1500 men were lost and the ocean beach was crowded with dead and dying, Harriet Tubman said, "Then we saw de lightening, and that was de guns; and then we heard de thunder, and that was de big guns; and then we heard de rain falling, and that was de drops of blood falling; and when we came to get in de crops, it was dead men that we reaped."

Harriet Tubman lived for a half-century after the Emancipation Proclamation was signed by President Lincoln and those for whom she cared so greatly were freed. Eventually the government granted her a meager pension of $20 a month. And from the book, "Harriet, the Moses of Her People," which Sarah H. Bradford wrote, came a little money. But, ever generous to a fault, Harriet Tubman died poor at the age of nearly a hundred. Poor but remembered—for the whole city of Auburn, New York, where she died went into mourning. And quite appropriately, her last rites as befitting a soldier of liberation, were military. At her funeral the local post of the Grand Army of the Republic presented the colors.

One of the most beautiful of tributes ever paid her came, however, from that other great fighter for the freedom of the slave, Frederick Douglass. In a letter to her some years before she died, he wrote:

"The difference between us is very marked. Most that I have done and suffered in the service of our cause has been in public and I have received much encouragement at every step of the way. You, on the other hand, have labored in a private way. I have wrought in the day—you in the night. I have had the applause of the crowd and the satisfaction that comes of being approved by the multitude, while the most that you have done has been witnessed by a few trembling, scared and footsore bondsmen and women whom you have led out of the house of bondage and whose heartfelt, *God bless you,* has been your only reward. The midnight sky and the silent stars have been the witnesses of your devotion to freedom and of your heroism."

Robert Smalls

1839-1915

Robert Smalls

PATRIOT

 1839-1915

Wʜᴇɴ Robert Smalls became famous as a Civil War hero, he was only twenty-three years old and a slave, the father of three children. They were little children, hardly aware as yet as to what slavery was. But Smalls did not want his offspring to remain slaves a moment longer than necessary, so he stole a Confederate gunboat and transported them into the waters of freedom. This daring exploit earned for him national recognition. And eventually Smalls became a Congressman from the very state in which he had been a slave.

Robert Smalls was born in Beaufort, South Carolina, in the Spring of 1839. His parents, Robert and Lydia, belonged to the McKee family there, a family with the reputation of treating their slaves well. They even allowed slave children to acquire a little education, so by the time young Robert was in his teens, he knew how to read and write. When his master moved to Charleston, Robert was hired out as a hotel waiter. But, having grown up near the sea, he was attracted to ships, and shortly he was permitted to work at the dockyards where he became a rigger. Sometimes, to his delight, he was allowed to take short trips outside Charleston Harbor. At seventeen Robert was allowed to marry a girl of his choice—a privilege not granted many slaves. And his life was a happy one in comparison to that of most other men in bondage.

But in spite of a lenient master, there was something about slavery that irked young Robert. For one thing, when Fort Sumter was fired on by the batteries of the new Confederacy and Charleston became its fortress, with no freedom of choice on his own part, Robert was impressed into the rebel service and forcibly assigned without pay to the crew of the *Planter*, a cotton transport hastily converted into an armed frigate by the Confederate Navy. The ship's commander, Captain Relay, and its two mates were, of course, white. But the sailors, firemen, and all the rest of the crew were Negro slaves. Robert Smalls became a fireman, stoking the boilers whenever the *Planter* ventured outside Charleston's waterways. Meanwhile, by watching the officers in charge of the ship, he learned all he could about navigation. Being a bright young man, Robert soon knew how to run the vessel himself and, if need be, could pilot it out of Charleston Harbor to the open sea.

The proud city of Charleston, a center of Southern wealth and culture, was one of the chief harbors during the war through which ammunition and supplies from abroad found their way to the Confederate rebels. This happened in spite of a Union blockade of the Eastern seaboard from Maryland to Florida. The North looked forward to capturing Charleston, although this was not easy. But the Union armies had early managed to take control of the nearby Sea Islands off the South Carolina and Georgia coasts, and to these islands flocked thousands of runaway slaves, or those liberated by the government forces. Hilton Head, Beaufort, and Port Royal were crowded with destitute freedmen—contrabands —who found even a hungry freedom preferable to bondage. Throughout the Union camps they sang:

Slavery chain done broke at last,
Broke at last, broke at last!
I'm gonna praise God till I die!

Or another song that they made up themselves often filled the air:

No more auction block for me,
No more, no more. . . .
No more driver's lash for me,
No more, no more.

Robert Smalls had heard of these centers of freedom only a short distance from Charleston, but to get to them through the rebel lines with his wife and children would be a dangerous and difficult thing to attempt. In normal times runaway slaves might be beaten within an inch of their lives. Now, in war time, they might be killed. In his mind Smalls began to conceive a plan of escape so bold that he hardly dared think about it. If the plan which he kept in the back of his head were successful, it would benefit not only himself and his family, but the Union cause as well. The scheme was simply to take charge of the *Planter* if and when such an opportunity came, place his family aboard and with himself at the helm, sail out of Charleston Harbor into the off-shore waters of the Union blockade fleet. This required not only great daring, but careful thinking as well.

Smalls knew that some nights when the ship was at dock, one or two of the white officers went to their homes in the city to sleep. If only some evening *all three* of them would go ashore for the night—the captain and both of his mates! For this eventuality, Smalls waited. Finally such a night came in the Spring of the second year of the War. On Monday, May 12, 1862, all three of the white officers of the *Planter* decided to go ashore to their families for the night. It was on this night that Smalls quietly rounded up his own family, his sister, and his brother John's wife and child. John himself was an engineer on the *Planter* and had already been taken into Robert's confidence. Together the two brothers decided to make their dash for freedom, taking not only their closest relatives, but the entire crew of Negro seamen with them. They made a group of sixteen in all.

They realized that by using the property of the Confederate government for escape—a vessel of the rebel navy—the penalties if captured would be severe. So these sixteen slaves agreed that if they were pursued and overtaken by Confederate gunboats, they would blow the *Planter* and themselves to bits. Failing in this, they would link their hands together and jump into the sea. All of them were willing to die attempting to be free. None meant to be taken alive. Charleston Harbor was full of ships and ringed by guardposts, so they were under no illusions as to the dangers involved. But their hopes were high, and the very audacity of Robert's plans gave them all courage. To sail away to freedom on a Confederate gunboat! They had to laugh at the idea of slaves doing such a thing. But that is just what they did.

While Captain Relay and his mates were at home that Monday sound asleep in their beds, soon after midnight by devious routes through darkened streets, the Negro women and children made their way to the wharf where the *Planter* lay. One by one they crept aboard and hid themselves in the hold. A few hours before dawn, Robert Smalls fired the boilers and soon the steam was up. Then he mounted the bridge and gave orders for the crewmen to cast off the ropes mooring the vessel to the dock, and to haul up the anchor. In the starry darkness Smalls raised the Confederate flag on the tallest mast and, with himself in charge, gave orders to sail. Everything was done as Captain Relay would do—for Small's plan was to make it appear that the *Planter* was leaving the harbor for early morning reconnoitering in the waters outside Charleston. And indeed, this is what the sentries on the docks must have thought as they saw the ship glide away from shore and steam slowly down the harbor through its ring of fortifications.

Deliberately, so as not to excite suspicion, the ship slid through the water. And, at each harbor post, Smalls gave the proper signal with a pull of the whistle cord. He had put on the captain's clothes and donned the same wide-brimmed straw hat that Relay wore when on deck. In the dark from a distance anyone might think it was Captain Relay himself on the bridge. The night was kind to Robert Smalls. He was short, stocky, brownskin, and looked nothing at all like the Confederate officer whose vessel he was so audaciously sailing away under the very noses of the harbor guns. But this young Negro's heart must have been in his mouth as the ship approached Fort Sumter, the heavily armed bastion at the mouth of the harbor. Suppose, for some unusual reason, orders came from the Fort to halt the vessel for inspection? What would happen then? Would the batteries of the Fort open fire on one of its own boats, if the ship did not stop? Smalls did not know. But fortunately such an eventuality did not come to pass. Calmly, as the *Planter* passed the Fort, Robert Smalls gave the accustomed signal on the whistle. The sentries, after what seemed like a very long time, called back, "Pass the *Planter!*" And the runaway ship went on to the open sea.

Manned by Negroes and carrying sixteen slaves dreaming of freedom, the *Planter* now sailed full steam ahead into the Atlantic. About the same time in the East the sky began to lighten as dawn came. Now out of range of the harbor guns, and well out of sight of the shore patrols, Robert Smalls hauled down the flag of the Confederacy and hoisted in its place a sheet taken from one of the bunks—a white flag of truce—and everyone aboard breathed easier. In the first gray light of morning, they sighted one of the Union vessels that was blockading the coast. The captain of the *Onward* recognized their flag of truce. And by the time the sun rose, Robert Smalls had turned over to the Union Navy the Confederate gunboat, *Planter*.

The Flag Officer of the Union Blockading Squadron, S. F. DuPont, sent at once to the Secretary of the Navy in Washington a report on the receipt of this prize of war, and in his report he praised Robert Smalls to the highest. He also recommended that Smalls and the members of his crew be awarded prize money for having delivered the *Planter*. Upon its passage, President Lincoln signed the measure. Money and honor. But greater than all to Smalls and his crewmen was the freedom that they found beneath the Union Jack.

Of his freedom Smalls made good use. Information which he supplied Union naval officers was described as "of the utmost importance." Apparently it was, since he is cited in an official report of the Secretary of the Navy to President Lincoln. According to this report, "From information derived chiefly from the contraband pilot, Robert Small, who has escaped from Charleston," the Union forces were able to occupy Stono and thus secure what the document describes as "an important base for military operations." Because of his general seamanship and his knowledge of the buoys and fortifications of Charleston Harbor, Smalls was appointed a pilot in the Quartermaster's Department of the United States Navy and, on the monitor *Keokuk*, he took part in an attack on

Fort Sumter. Later he was transferred to the *Planter* and, in December, 1863, when the commander of that vessel under Confederate fire deserted his post, Smalls took charge of the ship and steered it out of danger. For this, besides being cited for gallant and meritorious action, he was shortly promoted to the rank of Captain, and remained in the naval service for the duration of the War.

Meanwhile, Small's fame had spread throughout the state of South Carolina, and when the post-war reconstruction commenced, he became active in the political life of the region. In 1868 he was one of the members of the State Constitutional Convention convened to propose a new civil code and to rehabilitate the state's administration. For the former slave owners, including his own master, Smalls preached leniency, not vindication. In his heart there was no malice toward the past, only high hopes for the future of all, white and black, and the desire that they might work together for the good of the South. As a speaker Robert Smalls was fluent, self-possessed and convincing, commanding the respect of all who heard him. People of both races often referred to him as "the smartest colored man in South Carolina."

On January 1, 1863, as a war measure, Abraham Lincoln had signed the Emancipation Proclamation granting freedom to "all persons held as slaves within any State, or designated part of a State, the people whereof shall then be in rebellion against the United States." And in 1865 Congress, by the addition to the Constitution of the 13th Amendment, ended slavery everywhere in the United States. Some three and a half million bondsmen had then become free men, at a loss to the slave owners of over two billion dollars in human property values. In 1868 the 14th Amendment to the Constitution was passed granting the Negro full citizenship and declaring that no state should "deprive any person of life, liberty, or property without due process of law, nor deny to any person within its jurisdiction the equal protection of the laws." Lastly, in 1870 the 15th Amendment concerning suffrage was added to the Constitution. This stated that "The right of the citizens of the United States to vote shall not be denied or abridged by the United States or by any State on account of race, color, or previous condition of servitude."

These edicts were great steps forward in the processes of American democracy. But the former slave-holding states immediately sought ways of circumventing them. In some localities "Black Codes" were formulated which permitted Negroes to be indentured or apprenticed for long periods to white employers under conditions amounting to slavery. Curfew laws were instituted. Jury service was denied to blacks. And the Ku Klux Klan and other terrorist organizations came into being to prevent men of color from exercising their citizenship rights, particularly the right of the ballot. It became necessary for Federal troops to protect the polling places of the South. But, under such protection, for a while freedmen took an active part in Southern politics. It was during this period that Robert Smalls was elected to the South Carolina legislature, where for a time Negroes held the majority of the seats, since they constituted more than fifty per cent of the population. Since most freed Negroes were uneducated, they wanted education, and so they voted for free public schools for all. They wished protection for their own civil rights, so they sought such protection for all. In general colored office holders were influential in bringing about liberal and advanced legislation in many fields in the South.

For a number of years after the War, Robert Smalls was

an officer of the South Carolina State Militia in which he held various commissions. Being a staunch Republican, he became a delegate to several of that party's national conventions. And in 1875 he was sent as an elected representative from South Carolina to Washington where he served several terms, in all, a longer period in Congress than any other representative of color. After his congressional service, Smalls was appointed Collector of the Port of Beaufort, a post which he held for many years. After his retirement he lived in Beaufort until his death in 1813 at the age of seventy-four.

Of all the things that happened to Robert Smalls in his long and interesting life, perhaps none remained more vivid in his memory than a day when at the end of the War Between the States, as captain of the *Planter*—the ship on which he had escaped to freedom—he took part in the ceremony attending the raising of the Stars and Stripes once more over Fort Sumter. That day Captain Robert Smalls steered the *Planter* into Charleston Harbor, his mind and heart full of memories of the time when, a few years before, he had first taken command of the ship as a slave. Now on April 13, 1865, as the harbor guns boomed their salutes to victory, Smalls transported into Charleston a crowded shipload of jubilant Negroes from the Sea Islands, including the distinguished colored officer, Major Martin R. Delany and his soldier son of the famous 54th Massachusetts.

Boatloads of distinguished people from the North had come down for the victory ceremonies, including a number of famous abolitionists and almost the entire congregation of Henry Beecher's church in Brooklyn. Thousands of Negroes had gathered in Charleston, too. On the eve of the celebration at Michelville near Hilton Head outside the harbor of Charleston, in a crowded Negro church, William Lloyd Garrison, who had spent long years in the cause of freedom, rose to speak. The stirring Negro spirituals in wave after wave of joyous singing had already swept the congregation, and there were tears and cries of jubilation from the newly freed men and women packed into the building. And when they rose as one to greet Garrison, they were rising in salute to all the men and women, white and black, who had contributed to their freedom—from Lincoln and Garrison and Beecher to black Harriet Tubman, Frederick Douglass, and Charleston's own Robert Smalls whom they all knew so well. When the singing and crying had subsided, with a majestic passage from the Bible Garrison began his speech, "And Moses said unto the people, Remember this day in which ye came out from Egypt, out of the house of bondage . . . And it shall be when thy son asketh thee in time to come, saying, *What is this?* that thou shalt say unto him, By strength of hand the Lord brought us out of Egypt from the house of bondage . . . And it shall be for a token upon thine hand, and for frontlets between thine eyes: for by strength of hand the Lord brought us forth out of Egypt."

Robert Smalls and the steamship *Planter* are a part of the story of the Negro's heroic escape from the house of bondage.

Charles Young
1864-1922

Charles Young

WEST POINTER

～ 1864-1922 ～

Charles Young attained the highest rank accorded a Negro up to his time in the United States Army, that of colonel. Previously there had been a number of Negro officers of lesser rank, and in every war since the colonial period colored soldiers had taken part. Many were slaves impressed by their masters; others were runaways. Some were free men. They fought at Lexington and Concord, Ticonderoga, and the Battle of Bunker Hill in 1775. In 1776 when George Washington crossed the Delaware, Oliver Cromwell and Prince Whipple were with him, the latter in Washington's own boat. Tack Sisson took part in the raid on British headquarters at Newport in 1777. And that same year, history reports that at the height of the battle, "In the fight at Brandywine, Black Samson, a giant Negro armed with a scythe" swept through the ranks of the Redcoats. Paul Laurence Dunbar's poem about Samson asks:

> *Was he a freeman or bondsman?*
> *Was he a man or a thing?*
> *What does it matter? His brav'ry*
> *Renders him royal—a king.*

In some states slaves who served in the armed forces were granted their freedom at the war's end by legislative action, like those in Virginia after the revolution who had "contributed towards the establishment of American liberty and independence." It was during the Revolutionary War that the first American woman to wear a uniform saw official service as a soldier. She was a woman of color, Deborah Gannett, who disguised herself in a man's uniform and fought for a year and a half in the Fourth Massachusetts Regiment of the Continental Army under the name of Robert Shurtliff. For her courageous service, the State Legislature granted her a special monetary award with a citation that declared, "Deborah exhibited an extraordinary instance of female heroism."

In the War of 1812, after the Battle of New Orleans, General Andrew Jackson said of his Negro soldiers, "I expected much from you, but you have surpassed my hopes." And of the black sailors who then made up a sixth of the navy personnel on the Great Lakes, Commodore Perry said after the Battle of Lake Erie, "They seemed absolutely insensible to danger." And the commander of the *Governor Tompkins* declared that the name of one of his brave Negro seamen, John Johnson, deserved to be written high on the roll of fame.

In the War Between the States, fighting for their own liberty, almost two hundred thousand Negroes served in the Union Army or Navy. "The 62nd United States Colored Infantry," so it is recorded of the final skirmish in 1865 in Texas, "probably fired the last angry volley of the War, and Sergeant Crocket of that regiment received the last wound from a rebel hostile bullet, and hence shed the last fresh blood in the war resulting in the freedom of his race in the United States." All told, some 37,000 Negroes were killed in the service of the Union.

When the American battleship *Maine* in 1898 was sunk in Havana Harbor and the United States entered the war against Spain, the Twenty-Fourth and Twenty-Fifth Infantry and the Ninth and Tenth Cavalry were sent to Cuba. They saw action at San Juan, Las Guasimas, and El Caney, and other Negro units did occupation duty on the island after the war. At Santiago "for particularly meritorious service in the face of the enemy," four Negroes were commissioned lieutenants. And among the colored soldiers who are uniquely remembered in Cuba are thirty-five who volunteered to serve in experiments designed to check the yellow fever epidemics—and died as a result. It was in the Spanish-American War that Charles Young, then a major, took part.

Young was born on March 12, 1864, in the little village of Mayslick, Kentucky, but while still a youngster his parents moved to Ripley, Ohio. There Charles finished high school, and became a school teacher until, in 1884, he was appointed to the United States Military Academy at West Point. He was the ninth of his race to be admitted to this institution, but the large number of white Southern cadets made attendance there difficult for black students. Up to 1877 none had graduated. The first man of color to be graduated from West Point was Henry Ossian Flipper, born a slave in Georgia, who received his commission in that year; the next was John H. Alexander of Ohio in 1887; and in 1889 Charles Young was graduated. But in those days it was not easy for Negroes to get through West Point. Many fellow cadets would not speak to a colored classmate, and the usual indignities of hazings were doubled when it came to black plebes. But Young determined to stick it out, to perform his duties punctiliously, and to study hard. He came through successfully. At graduation Charles Young was commissioned a second lieutenant in the all-Negro unit, the Tenth Cavalry. After various transfers, he was assigned in 1894 as an instructor in Military Science at Wilberforce University, a Negro institution in Ohio. Then when the Spanish-American War began, he became a major in charge of the Ninth Ohio Regiment which was transferred to Cuba.

Race prejudice in high army circles often made life difficult for all-Negro troops. For example the Twenty-Fifth Infantry embarked on a government transport for Havana. But in the port of Tampa, Florida, when other soldiers were given individual shore leave, the Negro troops were not allowed off the boat except as a marching unit under white officers. They were assigned to the very bottom of the hold in hot and airless quarters, and were not permitted to mingle on deck with their white comrades in arms. But in spite of such discriminatory treatment, once in action the Negro soldiers fought gallantly. And at San Juan Hill the Ninth and Tenth Cavalries especially distinguished themselves.

In June, 1898, two white battalions of the First Volunteer Cavalry under the command of Colonel Theodore Roosevelt (who was later to become President of the United States) began at attack against the Spaniards on Santiago Ridge at Las Guasimas. Known as the Rough Riders, these troops of Teddy Roosevelt's had previously distinguished themselves in battle, but this time they found the going rough, particularly at San Juan Hill. The garrison of El Caney there was well fortified, and the slopes below it were a tangle of bushes, vines, and stunted trees through which had been strung treacherous barbed wire. The approaches to the slopes were marshlands. Blockhouses guarded the hillside and Spanish sharpshooters were concealed in the jungle undergrowth. Unaware of the enemy's strength and strategic positions, the white Rough Riders soon found themselves under dangerous fire from all sides. When the colored Ninth and Tenth Cavalry units, stationed some distance away, heard of their plight, the Negro soldiers quickly mounted horses and galloped to their aid, arriving just in time, dismounting to join the battle.

"Firing as they marched," a New York paper reported, "their aim was splendid, their coolness was superb, and their courage aroused the admiration of their comrades. . . . The war has not shown greater heroism." One of the white corporals in the fight later stated, "If it had not been for the Negro cavalry, the Rough Riders would have been exterminated." And another soldier said, concerning the aid of these mounted fighters which turned a possible defeat into victory, "Every one of us, from Colonel Roosevelt down, appreciates it." Certainly it was their strength that turned the tide of battle and contributed greatly to the battering into complete submission of the Spanish fort on the hilltop. Colonel Roosevelt himself added, "I don't think that any Rough Rider will ever forget the tie that binds us to the Ninth and Tenth Cavalry." And he repeated what one of the privates in his outfit had declared just after the battle, "They can drink out of our canteens."

After the Spanish-American War, Young served with military units in the Philippine Islands and in Haiti, then with General Pershing on the Mexican border. In 1915 in the punitive expeditions of American forces against Mexican guerrilla warriors across the border, a squadron of the Tenth Cavalry which Young commanded went to the rescue of Major Tompkins and his men when they were ambushed by the Mexicans near Parral. Young's bravery elicited wide newspaper comment. Shortly thereafter he was made a lieutenant colonel, and led numerous raids into the bandit-infested Mexican desert, seeking to dislodge the rebel leader, Pancho Villa.

But in spite of his military knowledge, his bravery, his

experience and his rank, when in April, 1917, the first World War involved the United States, Colonel Young was not assigned to European service. As the highest ranking Negro officer in the armed forces, his failure to see active duty proved a great disappointment to Negro Americans. They felt that the then existing race prejudice in our defense system prevented Colonel Young from being given service commensurate with his rank. At any rate, the army placed him on its list of officers to be retired, giving the cause as high blood pressure. However, to prove his physical fitness, Colonel Young rode all the way on horseback from his home in Xenia, Ohio, to the capital at Washington where he laid his case before Newton D. Baker, Secretary of War, but to no avail. Despondent because he would not be permitted to fight in the European theatre of war, Young mounted his horse and rode back to Ohio where he prepared his mind for retirement. But the retirement papers never came. Young was kept on the active list, but given no assignment. Then, when the war was almost over—in fact, just five days before the Armistice—Colonel Young was ordered to Camp Grant in Illinois to be in charge of trainees.

When the installations at Camp Grant were disbanded, Young was sent to Monrovia, Liberia, as a military attaché, one of his assignments being to aid in the reorganization of the Liberian Army. Colonel Young had a deep interest in African life and culture, and he spent his leisure hours gathering material for a book he hoped to write. He was a quiet man of varied interests, not purely military, and fond of composing both poetry and music in his spare time. He wrote a play called "The Military Morale of Races" and a book about Toussaint L'Ouverture, the leader of the Haitian slave revolts against the French. For his church in Xenia he made beautiful new arrangements of old hymns, and for concert use he composed eight serenades. Young played the piano well, also the cornet, and had acquired fluency in Spanish, French, and German. His few public appearances as a speaker drew large audiences, and he became a greater popular figure with Negro Americans who had followed his career with interest from the days of the Spanish-American War to his death in Nigeria in 1922.

Colonel Young had gone from Liberia to Lagos, the capital of Nigeria, on furlough. Expecting to use this great African city on the Niger River as a center, he intended to explore the surrounding territory in search of material for his book. On the way to the walled city of Kano whose civilization dates back to before Christ, Colonel Young became ill of fever and had to return to Lagos. There, on the coast of the African continent that he loved (he himself was of almost pure African descent), he died, an American soldier in a far off land—which happened to be the land of his ancestors. With appropriate military ceremonies, Colonel Charles Young was buried in the National Cemetery at Arlington where today a tall marble shaft marks his resting place.

Matthew A. Henson
1866-1955

Matthew A. Henson

EXPLORER

 **1866-1955**

THE North Pole was discovered on April 6, 1909, by Rear Admiral Robert E. Peary of the United States Navy. With Admiral Peary at the North Pole was the Negro, Matthew Henson. In fact, Henson was the trail breaker for Peary's expedition and, as such, went ahead first to the Pole, reaching it some forty-five minutes before the Admiral himself. So Henson was actually the very *first* man to stand at the top of the world.

At the Pole the latitude is 90 degrees North and from there all directions are South. In Admiral Peary's Log Book his arrival at the North Pole is recorded thus: "Arrived here today, 27 marches from Cape Columbia, I have with me 5 men, Matthew Henson, colored, Ootah, Eginwah, Seegloo, and Ookeah, Eskimos; 5 sledges and 38 dogs. The expedition under my command has succeeded in reaching the POLE . . . for the honor and prestige of the United States of America." To Henson then, his only English speaking companion, Peary is reported to have said, "This scene my eyes will never see again. Plant the Stars and Stripes over there, Matt—at the North Pole." His brown face seeming even browner in his hood of white fur, in a world of white ice and white snow, the Negro, Henson, planted the American flag at the very top of the earth.

Born on a farm in Charles County, Maryland, the year after the close of the War Between the States, Matthew Alexander Henson had a harsh childhood. When he was two years old, his mother died and his father married again. But Matt was only eight when his father died, too. His stepmother was not kind to him. She made him work very hard, would not even allow him to go to school, and often whipped him severely. So when he was eleven years old, in the middle of the winter, Matt decided to run away. While everyone else was asleep in the house, in the dark of night he started out on foot, heading toward Washington, a city he had often heard of but was not sure of its location. Eventually the little boy got to Washington by himself. A kind colored woman who ran a small lunch room took him in, fed him, and gave him a job as her dishwasher at a dollar and a half a week. For a number of years he was happy, until the urge came over him to travel further. In Baltimore Matt had heard there were docks and great ships that sailed away into all the waters of the world. Young Henson wanted to become a sailor.

He was lucky. After walking from Washington to Baltimore, it was not long before the thirteen-year-old youth found a job on a boat, a square-rigger with tall white sails destined for Hong Kong, a port half way around the world. Matt was signed on as a cabin boy. Added to this good fortune was the fact that the *Katie Hines* was in command of a kind-hearted captain who took an interest in the brave Negro youngster who could hardly read or write. The captain decided to teach him to read and write well before the ship got back to Baltimore. In those days it was a voyage of many months to China. Every day the captain gave him a private class in his cabin, and in this way Matt acquired the ground-work of a good education on a windjammer rocking and rolling through the troughs of the sea.

For five years Matt Henson sailed on the *Katie Hines*, learning seamanship, learning from books, learning from people of all nationalities, and growing into a man. One entire winter the ship was locked in by ice at the Russian harbor of Murmansk, where Matt learned to speak Russian, hunt wolves, and drive sleighs. Later he saw the pagodas of Japan, the gypsies of Spain, the palm trees of the West Indies, and the great rivers of Africa. Matt picked up a smattering of many languages, and some he learned well. He acquired a knowledge and understanding of strange peoples and strange ways, and learned to take foreign customs in his stride and to mingle amiably with everybody. This ability to get along with strangers and live with folks whose language he did not speak, stood him in good stead later in life, for it was his destiny to become an explorer. The good captain of the *Katie Hines*, who introduced the world to Matt, died when he was seventeen. His ship had just left Jamaica heading through the Caribbean for Baltimore. With the Captain in his cabin when he died was the boy he had guided toward manhood, young Matthew Henson. The master of the ship was buried at sea.

Matt did not sail on the *Katie Hines* again. He shipped instead on a fishing boat, but quit when it reached Newfoundland. In Boston and other cities along the coast as far as New York, young Henson worked at various jobs ashore—nightwatchman, ditch digger, coachman. Then when he was nineteen he went back to Washington again. There, two years later, working as a stockroom clerk in a men's furnishing store, he met young Robert Peary, a civil engineer for the Navy, who came in to the store to buy a sun helmet for use in the tropics. Peary offered Matt Henson a job as his personal attendant on a surveying trip to Nicaragua for the government. Henson did not like the idea of being anyone's man-servant, but he felt intuitively that the job might lead to something better. Having adventure in his blood, he accepted it. In no time at all, Peary recognized in the young Negro qualities of value far beyond those of a personal servant, so he promoted him to his surveying crew as a field helper. For twenty-three years thereafter, Henson was associated with Peary in his work and his trips.

Peary was not a rich man so he could not always personally afford to pay Henson for his services. But on their return from Central America, a job was secured for Henson on government pay as a messenger in Peary's office at the Navy Yard in Philadelphia. About a year later, Peary told young Henson about a proposed expedition to Greenland. He intended to explore the northern icecaps, and he said he desired very much to take him along. But since the trip had very meager backing, there was no money to pay for Henson's services. Matt Henson volunteered to go without pay. In this he was joined by a number of adventuresome whites, all imbued with the spirit of exploration rather than gain. In 1888 they set out for Baffin Bay. In spite of the fact that Peary suffered a broken leg shortly after his arrival in Greenland, he and the whole party elected to allow their ship to depart, leaving them isolated for a year at the foot of a glacier they hoped to cross.

Matt built a house for Peary, his wife, and the rest of the party and aided in the construction of sledges for their inland trips. From the Eskimos, he learned how to handle a team of eight to sixteen dogs to pull sledges across the ice. Matt's light tan skin at first caused the Eskimos to think him one of them, but speaking another tongue. In short order he had established friendly relations with the native peoples and soon began to learn their language. That winter they taught him a great many things useful to know in the frozen North, especially how to hunt, trap, and fish for food. Since Henson put his newly acquired knowledge at the disposal of the entire party of explorers, he became a most valuable man to Peary's expedition. Lieutenant Peary realized his value and respected Henson accordingly. Matt, in turn, sympathized deeply with Peary's aims and marvelled at his determination. Soon between the two men there sprang up a relationship of mutual admiration and dependence. Finally, when the party set out in the face of stinging sleet through sub zero weather to conduct its explorations, Matt was considered one of the most important men in the group. By then, on the part of others, his race had been entirely forgotten. Here in the frozen North, no one thought of color lines. In the primitive Arctic, a man was a man—and that was that. When the expedition returned to New York in 1892, Peary told Matt Henson, "We are going back to the Arctic again—but next time, all the way to the North Pole."

At the turn of the century, no one knew what lay at either the North Pole or the South Pole. At the earth's axis would there be snow-covered land, or only drifting ice floes impossible of crossing? Nobody could tell. And how could a man reach the North Pole? By land or by sea? No one knew. In those days there were no radios to keep up communications with the rest of the world. There was no aviation to survey terrain from the air, or planes to drop food were explorers to be stranded, or to effect a quick rescue if men were isolated. To make an attempt to reach the North Pole, anyhow, was considered by most people to be a foolhardy adventure indeed. But Henson and Peary both wanted to attempt it. They did.

A party of eleven men and two women again headed for Greenland, with Peary intending to go further North this time. But, after a year of Arctic hardships and frustrations, all but two of the men returned to the United States. Only Matt Henson and one other stuck by Peary, electing to remain another year, sticking out a second winter that they might go forward in the spring. Peary's first attempt that year to reach the Pole had been unsuccessful, and their supplies were buried in a frozen drift of snow and ice. In April 1896, another attempt was made in the face of icy winds that bore down from the North under the cold but continuous glare of a twenty-four-hour sun on blindingly white snow. In their three dog-sledges, the men often lost contact in the swirling blizzards through which they travelled. It was slow and dangerous going over ice that might split and isolate one dog team from another. Finally the third man, Lee, was lost. Peary and Henson made camp trusting he would catch up to them but he did not. To keep warm while waiting and hoping, the two men slept huddled in furs as close together as they could, that their body heat might keep each other from freezing. After three days Henson went in search of the third man and luckily found him. But Lee was almost frozen on top of his dog sledge though still alive. Henson rescued him and treated him for frostbite and extreme exposure. When their food supply got so low the men could not share any of it with the dogs, they would each day kill a dog and feed that one to the other animals. Finally, the men were reduced to eating dogs themselves. After a month, however, the three pioneers had covered six hundred miles.

But they were too exhausted by then and their supplies too low to hope to go any further and expect ever to make the long trek back to civilization alive. Besides, scurvy, the dreaded disease caused by malnutrition, set in. They had failed.

But they brought back to New York from the Greenland coast two large meteorites of scientific interest, leaving behind one of many tons that was too large to be loaded aboard their small ship. In 1896 Peary and Henson returned to Cape York to get this gigantic fallen meteor but again failed to dislodge it from the ice to haul it aboard ship, so they returned to the States without their prize. But in 1897 they secured a larger ship and stronger tackle, sailed again to Greenland and this time brought back to New York the largest meteorite in the world which gained Peary wide newspaper publicity as well as a profitable lecture tour. Matt, meanwhile, was employed by the American Museum of Natural History as an assistant in the mounting of Arctic animals and arranging true-to-nature panoramas of the beasts and backgrounds of the far North. In England Peary's lectures and interviews were so successful that a publisher presented him with a ship, the *Windward*, especially equipped for Arctic travel. On his return to America, he immediately began to plan another Polar search, this time working out details most carefully in advance, selecting a full complement of assistants to cover each lap and preparing to spend at least four years on the expedition. He alerted Matt to be ready to accompany him.

Off again in 1898, Peary and Henson steamed past the Statue of Liberty but ice prevented the *Windward* from penetrating as far north as Peary had hoped. They got only to Cape d'Urville on Ellesmere Island. From there Peary decided to go by sledge overland to Fort Conger, deserted fifteen years before by another exploring party which had left behind a large stock of supplies. This trip to Conger was one of two hundred and fifty miles through deep snowdrifts over mountains of ice but Matt and Peary, with a group of Eskimos, got there. On arrival, Peary's feet were frozen so badly that some of his toes snapped off as his shoes were removed. For three months at Conger, Matt cared for Peary, treating his frozen feet and trying to prevent gangrene from setting in. When they could travel again, they returned to Cape d'Urville where all of Peary's remaining toes, except one on either foot, had to be amputated. This great misfortune left him a partial cripple for life. Convalescence did not keep him from remaining for two years more in Greenland but again he failed on this trip to reach the Pole. At Etah, Matt and Peary passed many months alone, except for the Eskimos and they were the first men finally to define for map makers the northern rim of Greenland. When they returned to New York in 1902, they had added to the geographical knowledge of the world by this major exploration.

Over a period of many years, from youth to middle-age, the still determined Robert Peary made a total of eight unsuccessful attempts to reach the Pole and on all but one Matt Henson accompanied him. Henson became an expert in his knowledge of the Arctic and its winds and weather. In the frozen North, far away from the centers of civilization, he developed into a sort of Jack-of-all-trades since there was nothing Matt would not do to be of value to himself or his party. He learned to harpoon walrus; to hunt reindeer, bear and musk-oxen; to skin and stuff animals; to cook over a hole in the ice and to build igloos as an ice shelter against zero gales. He could not only build a boat but navigate it.

He could interpret for the white men and the Eskimos. He was so good at manipulating heavily loaded dog sledges even in blizzards of 50 degrees below that Peary once said of Henson, "He is a better dog driver and can handle a sledge better than any man living except some of the best Eskimo hunters themselves." With the Eskimos no one could form closer friendships or achieve their cooperation more quickly than could Henson. He not only learned to speak their language but to understand their jokes, eat their food and wear their clothes. He adopted an orphan Eskimo boy, Kudlooktoo. And once when Henson slipped on an ice floe and went into the freezing water, it was an Eskimo who pulled him out and saved his life.

On the expedition begun in 1905, they went by ship as far as Cape Sheridan, then by sledge and on foot across the ice of the Polar Sea. That year Peary and Matt Henson reached a new fartherest North, 87°6″, only 175 miles from the Pole. Here again they were stymied by all the conditions that make travel in the Land of the Midnight Sun excessively difficult—the breaking ice floes, the towering cliffs of frozen snow, the swirling blizzards and the terrors of complete isolation. With supplies gone, dogs emaciated and the Eskimos exhausted, for days they faced death on floating ice fields as they tried to make their way back to their base camp. Again defeated, Matt and Peary reached New York on Christmas Eve, 1906. The following year Henson got married.

But marriage did not keep Matt at home when the call came again to seek with the undaunted Peary a foothold at the top of the world. Two more determined men than Peary and Henson have never been known in the annals of exploration. One disappointment after another plus the ridicule of the press of the world at his continual failures only made Peary more adamant in his ambition to reach 90 degrees North where no man had ever stood before. On each expedition his accompanying members changed but Matt Henson remained with him. Henson was forty-two years old when again he left the United States on July 8, 1908, once more heading for familiar Cape Sheridan. This time President Roosevelt came aboard their ship in New York harbor to see the expedition off and to cheer its departure. Matt Henson's wife was at the pier, too, and he took her kiss with him to the Arctic.

Leaving the ship at Cape Sheridan, they travelled over-land ninety-three miles across the snow to Cape Columbia where a base was established. From here across seas of ice it was four hundred uncharted miles to the Pole and the temperature was so cold that often the men's beards were frozen stiff from the moisture from their breath. Eighteen years of determination lay behind Peary when on February 28, 1909 he began another attempt to reach the Pole. Beyond the rim of the endless day that at that time of year lights the North, his goal lay. They got off to a good start. But in March a great lead of water that they could not cross—an Arctic river between the ice—stopped their progress and made it ap-pear they might never get further. Fortunately, after a week of waiting, the weather went even further below zero. Then the lead froze permitting lightly loaded sledges to cross and re-cross conveying supplies to the other side. When they were a hundred and thirty miles from the Pole, the last of the supporting parties received orders to turn back. Now Peary and Henson were left alone with the Eskimos for their final dash Northward—one Negro man and one white man des-tined, if successful, to make history. They had with them four Eskimos, five sledges and a group of husky dogs. Matt was to blaze the trail, Peary to follow.

A gruelling trail it was over a white wilderness of snow and ice, but they pushed forward. "Day and night were the same," wrote Henson later in his autobiography, *A Negro at the North Pole*. "My thoughts were on the going and the getting forward and on nothing else. The wind was from the southeast and seemed to push us on and the sun was at our backs, a ball of livid fire rolling his way above the horizon in never ending day." But on this last lap, he continued, "As we looked at each other we realized . . . the time had come for us to demonstrate that we were the men who, it had been ordained, should unlock the door which held the mystery of the Arctic."

By April 5 they were thirty-five miles from the Pole. Peary with his mutilated feet was then fifty-three years old and Matt was no longer young either. Could it be that at last their dream of so many years would come true? That night only the Eskimos slept—uninterested in seeking a new spot of ice in this world of ice they had known all their lives. Henson and Peary could not sleep for the excitement of it. A part of Matt's job as trailblazer was to build an igloo of ice at each stopping point so that when Peary got there they could rest until time to start again. On the day when Henson, forging ahead, finally arrived at a point where North no longer existed, he knew he had reached the Pole. With Ootah's assistance, there he began to build an igloo. Forty-five minutes later, with Eskimos and a team of dogs, Peary arrived. To Matt Henson, Peary gave the honor of planting the American flag at the North Pole while he stood in salute. It was April 6, 1909.

Eleven years later Admiral Peary died, but Matt Henson lived to be eighty-eight years old. He passed away in New York City in 1955. In tribute to his long series of explorations, Matt Henson received a Congressional Medal, a gold medal from the Chicago Geographical Society, a loving cup from the Bronx Chamber of Commerce and a building has been named after him at Dillard University. On the occasion of the forty-fifth Anniversary of the Discovery of the North Pole, President Eisenhower honored Matt Henson at the White House.

Ida B. Wells

 1869-1931

Ida B. Wells

CRUSADER

 1869-1931

IDA B. WELLS was born in Holly Springs, Mississippi, a
few years after the close of the War between the North and
South. She grew to be a pretty little girl, slight, nut-brown,
delicate of features. And she became a very beautiful young
woman. To look at her, refined and ladylike in manner,
lovely as a flower, no one would think that she was destined
to become a defier of mobs and a vigorous crusader against
all the brutalities that beset the Negro people in the Post-
Reconstruction days in the South. But Ida B. Wells felt that
all of the rights vouchsafed American citizens in the Constitution of the United States, should belong to Negro citizens,
too, particularly the right to the protection of life and liberty
from mob violence. In Mississippi as a child little Ida saw
the white-robed Ku Klux Klan ride through the night to
frighten defenseless colored people away from the polls. She
heard of the burning of Negro schools, and of Negro homes
—if the owners happened to become too prosperous to suit the
members of the Klan. These things Ida B. Wells thought
wrong, undemocratic and uncivilized.

To better combat the evils of bigotry that she saw around
her, even as a child Ida knew she had to acquire education. So

when her parents were stricken with yellow fever and she found herself saddled early in life with the care of her younger brothers and sisters, she determined nevertheless to remain in school. First she attended Rust College in her home town, Holly Springs, then she went to Fisk University in Nashville where she wrote for the campus magazine. While still in her teens Ida became a country school teacher. Eventually she got an appointment in the public schools of Memphis and at the same time she began to write a column for a colored newspaper there. Intrigued by journalism and realizing the power of the printed word, she invested the money she earned from teaching in a paper called the *Memphis Free Speech* of which she became a co-owner and the editor.

In the South at that time there were still white people who wished to see Negroes back in slavery. Many who did not go so far as this in their desires, still did not want, under any circumstances, to grant black men and women equal civil rights, or permit them to vote. Such persons had little use for Negro newspapers, especially if they spoke out against the abuses and illegalities forced upon the colored people. But as an editor Ida B. Wells could not keep silent in the face of the almost daily violence and intimidation then prevalent in Tennessee and surrounding states. For decades after the War, the Mississippi Delta was troubled by racial strife. Lynchings and violent incidents of the ugliest sort were commonplace, with the courts unwilling to convict their perpetrators when the victims of violence were colored. Under the editorship of the young Miss Wells, the pages of *Free Speech* blazed with indignation against such a state of affairs where not even the humblest and most subservient Negroes might feel reasonably safe as to life, liberty, or even the expectation of the pursuit of happiness.

More than once, because of her outspokenness in print, Ida B. Wells received threats against her life and against her newspaper. To continue to write and publish her editorials opposing bigotry and violence, took a great deal of heroism on the part of this pretty young woman who looked too fragile to lift anything heavier than a pen in self-defense. But Joan of Arc in France had not been a big woman either, so Ida had read, but Joan had been brave, and she had stood up against armies for what she believed. Ida B. Wells was not afraid to stand up against mobs. But that any man or woman should have to do so in the United States was, she felt, the great shame of the times. To help wipe out this shame of racial prejudice, she decided to dedicate her life to stirring people into action against it. It was this dedication that eventually caused her to be driven out of Memphis.

When in 1877 at the end of the Reconstruction period, Federal troops were withdrawn from the South, the recently freed Negroes were left unprotected at the mercy of local prejudices. Their civil rights were violated at will, and in some communities black people were not even allowed to walk on the sidewalks. One petition in 1888 from Negroes in the Deep South which was printed in the Congressional Record declared that "unarmed and unable to offer resistance to an overpowering force which varies from a 'band of white' to a 'sheriff's posse' or the 'militia'," Negroes in the Delta were being "whipped and butchered when in a defenseless condition." Aside from the other forms of violence, there were in the South that year 137 recorded lynchings. The following year there were 170. And in the decade from 1890 to 1900, 1,217 Negroes met their deaths without trial through mob violence.

Just across the Mississippi River from Memphis where

Ida B. Wells lived, conditions for Negroes in 1892 in Arkansas were so frightful that an appeal was sent to Northern newspapers for help. It read in part, "People all over the state are being lynched upon the slightest provocation; some being strung up to telegraph poles, others burnt at the stake and still others being shot like dogs. In the last thirty days there have been not less than eight colored persons lynched in this state. At Texarkana a few days ago, a man was burnt at the stake. In Pine Bluff a few days later two men were strung up and shot. . . . Over in Toneoke County a whole family, consisting of husband, wife and child, were shot down like dogs. Verily the situation is alarming in the extreme. . . . The white press of the South seems to be subsidized by this lawless element, the white pulpits seem to condone lynching. The colored press in the South is dared to take an aggressive stand against lynch law. The Northern press seems to care little about the condition of Negroes in the South. The pulpits of the North are passive. Will not some who are not in danger of their lives, speak out against . . . lynchings and mob violence? For God's sake, say or do something, for our condition is precarious in the extreme."

It was in a moral climate such as this that Ida B. Wells, then only twenty-three years old, published her paper and composed her editorials. Those men and women who, surrounded by decent people in their own communities, protest against evils in *far away* places, are not necessarily brave people. But men and women who stand *in the midst* of evil and fight it, especially in the face of physical danger, have within them the qualities of heroism. In Memphis Ida B. Wells knew that to protest mob violence was dangerous. But protest she must—and did. History remembers her heroism.

Early in the month of March in the year 1892 in Memphis, three young Negro businessmen were dragged from jail at night by a masked mob and riddled with bullets in a field just outside the city. Most of the members of the mob were well known to the community at large, but none were punished for these mass murders. The Negroes killed—Calvin McDowell, William Stewart, and Thomas Moss—were not hoodlums, but intelligent, clean-cut, ambitious young men, respected by all who knew them. Their violent and unwarranted deaths, said to have been instigated by white business competitors, almost touched off a race riot on the part of the Negro citizens of Memphis, so deeply hurt and angered were they by the lack of police protection which permitted this atrocious deed to happen. In her paper Ida B. Wells published a full account of the tragic affair, naming those said to have been among the mob, and pointing the finger of blame at lackadaisical city officials. Immediately her life was threatened. And the night after that week's edition of *Free Speech* appeared on the newsstands, a mob invaded its plant, destroyed its printing presses, and burnt the remaining papers. Then they went in search of the editor. But friends had spirited her from the city. Openly the whites threatened to lynch her if she returned. Ida B. Wells was forced out of Memphis.

She came North and secured work on a Negro newspaper in New York City, *The Age*, to which often she had sent dispatches before leaving Memphis. Its editor, T. Thomas Fortune, himself a distinguished journalist and good friend of Booker T. Washington, said of the new young writer on his staff, "She has plenty of nerve and is as sharp as a steel trap." In New York Miss Wells met the great Frederick Douglass, the Harvard graduate, Monroe Trotter, a militant Boston editor, and other prominent colored men and women of that day. All of them took an interest in this daring young woman from the South. They encouraged her in her plans for bringing Southern conditions to the attention of the American public, aided her in getting lecture engagements, and donated funds for the collecting and publication of data on lynchings. In 1895 Ida B. Wells published the first carefully compiled statistical record of lynchings in the United States, a pamphlet entitled, *The Red Record*. And she became one of the leaders of a growing movement among liberals in the North to put an end to mob violence in America.

In 1898 she personally petitioned President McKinley at the White House to take action against mob law. She discussed with him the recent lynching of a United States postmaster in Florida. And respectfully the President listened as she added, "Nowhere in the civilized world save the United States of America do men, possessing all civil and political power, go out in bands of fifty to five thousand to hunt down, shoot, hang or burn to death a single individual, unarmed and absolutely powerless. Statistics show that nearly 10,000 American citizens have been lynched in the past twenty years. To our appeals for justice the stereotyped reply has been that the government could not interfere in a state matter. . . . We refuse to believe this country, so powerful to defend its citizens abroad, is unable to protect its citizens at home. Italy and China have been indemnified by this government for the lynching of their citizens. We ask that the government do as much for its own."

As a platform crusader against race prejudice and lynch law, Ida B. Wells became immensely popular not only in her own country but abroad. Of her lecture campaigns in Great Britain, a prominent churchman said, "Nothing since the days of Uncle Tom's Cabin has taken such a hold in England as the anti-lynching crusade." Quite correctly, Miss Wells did not entirely blame the South for mob evils. She once said, "Is not the North by its seeming acquiescence as responsible morally as the South is criminally for the awful lynching record of the past thirteen years? When I was first driven from Memphis, Tennessee, and sought a hearing in the North to tell what the Negro knew from actual experience of the lynching mania . . . not a newspaper to which I made application would print the Negro side of this question." And even in the North, free speech for Ida B. Wells was not always secure. She was not infrequently heckled from the audience, and sometimes physically threatened by bigots who did not like to see any colored person ask for the rights of democracy.

In 1895 Ida B. Wells married another crusader, a Chicago newspaper man, Ferdinand L. Barnett, and together they continued their campaign for equal rights for Negro Americans. They broadened the field of their activities, too, to include every social problem of importance in the Windy City where they lived. A great organizer of clubs, youth groups, and civic leagues, Ida Wells Barnett, as she was known in later life, continued active nationally, travelling throughout the Middle West and East, and sometimes into the South for speeches. She was among the six Negro signers of the initial call that resulted in a great national conference on Negro problems in New York in 1909, and out of which eventually grew the powerful National Association for the Advancement of Colored People, destined to play a most influential role in affairs relating to race in our country.

Active until the end, Ida Wells Barnett died in Chicago in the spring of 1931 after an illness of only two days. Now there stands in that city a large low-rent housing development bearing her name, and in many cities throughout the country there are women's clubs christened in her honor. At her death the *Chicago Defender* described her as the people of that city remembered her toward the end of her life: "Elegant, striking, always well groomed . . . regal." The work of keeping a statistical record of lynchings which she began, was carried on by Tuskegee Institute. But, fortunately, that particular form of mob violence diminished so greatly in the United States until in 1951 there was only one lynching. And since the year 1951 none has been officially recorded. Many feel that Ida B. Wells' long life devoted to the eradication of lynching, no doubt, helped to put an end to that evil.

Hugh N. Mulzac

1886-

Hugh N. Mulzac

MASTER MARINER

᪥ 1886- ᪥

CAPTAIN HUGH NATHANIEL MULZAC is listed in "Who's Who in Colored America" as a master of ocean going steamships unlimited. He was born near the sea in Kingston on the island of St. Vincent in the British West Indies. There he attended the Church of England School. In his early twenties, looking forward to a career on the sea in Great Britain he enrolled at Swansea Nautical College in South Wales. In 1911 young Mulzac settled in the United States and shortly thereafter became an American citizen. He attended the Shipping Board School in New York. Between ocean voyages on which he gained his practical experience, Mulzac studied navigation and wireless techniques. By 1920 he was ready to take the examinations as a ship's master, and that year he received his papers. In 1922 he became the captain of the S.S. *Yarmouth* of the Black Star Line belonging to the Back-to-Africa organization of a famous Negro leader, Marcus Garvey. During his years at sea, Mulzac circled the globe fifteen times and visited nearly every major port on earth. But it was during World War II as the master of the Liberty Ship *Booker T. Washington* that Captain Mulzac became famous. Dodging submarines, his ship transported safely across the Atlantic

18,000 soldiers and prisoners, as well as thousands of tons of war material, without the loss of a single man.

Some 24,000 Negroes served in all capacities in the United States Merchant Marine during the War. The racial discrimination that had formerly prevailed on most American ships, both civilian and naval, when colored seamen were relegated largely to jobs as messmen, under wartime conditions gradually disappeared,—partially in the navy and on merchant vessels almost entirely. The influential National Maritime Union, a large liberal organization, threw its weight against outmoded color lines in employment at sea, and President Roosevelt's Executive Order 8802 against discrimination in wartime contracts helped too. The result was that by the end of the war there were not only Negro seamen on deck but colored engineers in the engine room, wireless men in the radio cabin, and Negro officers on the bridge. Colored Americans of other minority groups were also employed in increasing numbers. In Captain Mulzac's crews there were whites, Negroes, Filipinos, and Chinese-Americans. Among the many new cargo vessels built especially for wartime voyages, fourteen were named after outstanding Negroes, and four for colored sailors who had sacrificed their lives in the service. Two such Liberty Ships, the *Frederick Douglass* and the *Robert L. Vann*, were sunk by the Germans.

As a teenager in the West Indies, Hugh Mulzac signed on a Norwegian sailing vessel for his first voyage, other than little trips from island to island on small boats in the Caribbean. The first foreign port at which he set foot ashore was Wilmington, North Carolina, and it was there that the Negro youth first experienced discrimination. With the Norwegian captain of his ship, Hugh went to church on Sunday morning. But because he was brown of skin, the ushers would not admit him to the church whose congregation was white. So the Captain refused to go into the services, also, declaring that Jesus Christ couldn't possibly be inside a church where all were not welcome.

From the United States the ship crossed to England, and there young Mulzac had a chance to see all the historic sites of London that he had read about in school. He had been a serious student who liked books as well as travel and adventure. He tried to read good books about all the countries he visited during his succeeding years at sea—from Europe to Australia, India and China, to South America. By the time he was twenty-five years old, Mulzac's knowledge of seamanship and harbors was sufficient for him to be granted a second mate's license for both sailing and steam vessels.

When the First World War began, Hugh Mulzac was shipping out of Baltimore, for in that city he had married and established a home. As a Second Mate he made a number of voyages to England and France on ships carrying war materials to the Allies, and in Baltimore he attended the War Shipping Board School for the training of officers desiring upgrading. Mulzac then took the examinations for Chief Mate and passed. Then in 1920 he appeared before the Merchant Marine Inspectors in Baltimore as a candidate for master's papers, and came through the examination with a very high rating. But, in those days, it was unheard of for a Negro to captain an American ship, so the young man was forced to continue to sail as a mate until after the war when Marcus Garvey made him captain of the Negro-owned *Yarmouth*, steaming between New York and the West Indies. During the Depression, however, this ship was docked, so for a time Captain Mulzac conducted a school for the training of seamen. Later he himself went back to sea, taking whatever positions his color would permit him to hold, from steward to mate to wireless operator. But he was blacklisted by shipowners after taking part in a strike, and so was compelled again to seek work ashore, this time as a house painter.

When World War II broke out in Europe and all seamen were badly needed, Mulzac shipped on a boat carrying war materials to the British in Egypt. Nazi planes and subs forced the ship to go all the way around the tip of Africa, rather than through the Mediterranean. More than once Mulzac knew what it was to be bombed by the Germans. After two such trips for the British, when the United States entered the war Captain Mulzac applied to the War Shipping Administration to offer his services as master of one of the new vessels then being built by the government. He also placed applications as a ship's master with every steamship line in New York. But, even though they were crying for experienced officers, because of his color, no company would employ Mulzac as a master. Elderly white captains were being called out of retirement to take charge of vessels under dangerous wartime conditions of a sort such as many of them had never experienced. Mulzac had sailed through the First World War, but was being denied the chance of sailing in the Second.

Finally, after great pressure from Negro organizations, the National Maritime Union, other powerful labor groups, and the intervention of President Roosevelt's Committee on Fair Employment Practices, Mulzac was offered the captaincy of a new Liberty ship, the *Booker T. Washington,* then about to be launched in California. But he was told that he must gather an all-Negro crew for this boat. Not only would such a segregated crew have been against union policies, but it certainly was against Mulzac's own beliefs, since he felt that all seamen should work together, regardless of race. Therefore, Captain Mulzac refused to accept the ship under conditions which stipulated that his crew should be composed only of Negroes. He stuck to his point and in the end won the privilege of choosing the members of his crew from among any competent seamen who might apply for berths on the *Booker T. Washington.* When the ship took to the sea on October 15, 1942, almost half of the crewmen were white, the others colored. And all during the war years, there was no nationality barrier on Captain Mulzac's ship. So successfully did this vessel operate—the first in the American Merchant Marine to be captained by a Negro—that soon three other Liberty ships were commissioned with colored masters, commanding crews of their choice.

Southward through the Pacific to the Panama Canal and then into the Caribbean, Captain Mulzac took his new ship on her maiden voyage, then up the East Coast to New York. There the Greater New York Council of CIO Unions had prepared a banquet of welcome for this ship and its crew, and it was hailed as an inspiring example of the fact that whites and Negroes could easily work together without difficulties on an American vessel. The souvenir program of the banquet stated:

The *Booker T. Washington* is more than a ship. It's crew heralds the people's unity which victory over the Axis will bring. These seamen, from 18 of the United Nations and 13 States of our Union, are America's answer to Jim Crow and Fascist race theories. On this new Liberty Ship, a floating symbol of our war aims, these brave sailors are proving that men of all races and colors can live and work together in harmony and concord and fight together for a world free from intolerance and oppression.

At this banquet, with the four stripes of gold of a Master Mariner on his shoulders, when Captain Mulzac rose to speak he was cheered.

After its New York reception, the *Booker T. Washington* headed for Halifax where it was to await convoy company through the submarine infested waters to Europe. From Nova Scotia on, the captain and his men would face all the dangers of modern warfare from both above and below the seas, at the mercy of planes as well as U-boats. And in winter the towering tons of water that compose the mighty waves of the North Atlantic, along with the thousand-mile gales that blow, may be as dangerous in their impact as any man-made explosives. Just off the coast of Newfoundland, the *Booker T. Washington* encountered a terrific storm that battered her so badly she lost her place for a time in the convoy. Then, once back with the other ships, some of the cargo on the piled-high deck broke loose in a storm, endangering the entire boat, for shifting cargo can cause a vessel to sink. Again Mulzac had to drop behind the rest of the ships, and this time he lost them altogether. Quite alone now, through perilous waters, the *Booker T. Washington* had to make its own way into port. Mulzac steered for Ireland, and in spite of enemy wolf packs, he reached there safely. The only shot fired at his ship was from a patrol boat guarding the port of entry. The officers were not accustomed to sighting a lone vessel coming into harbor in wartime, so it was mistaken for a possible enemy ship off its course. So dramatic was this first voyage of the first merchant steamer captained by a colored man, that it was dramatized and broadcast nationally in the United States.

Between 1942 and 1947, the *S.S. Booker T. Washington* made twenty-two round trips between the United States and

various ports of the battle areas, running the gauntlet of submarines and planes, gliding at night without lights through
the Mediterranean blockade, and sometimes limping into port
battered by waves, or with a part of its substructure shattered
by a torpedo. Yet somehow this ship always managed to
make it, even when the waters were shaken by explosives all
about it. Some of its seamen said their boat lead a charmed
life—*just lucky*—while others credited the skill and judg-
ment of their intrepid captain with keeping them out of the
most serious jams. Certainly the officers and men on Captain
Mulzac's ship had great faith in his ability and there was
comparatively little turnover among the personnel of his
ship. Mulzac took a deep personal interest in his crewmen,
himself conducting a class in navigation for all who wanted
to attend, and holding a ship meeting in the Officers Saloon
every Sunday for licensed and unlicensed men alike. At such
meetings anyone from the humblest messboy up to mates and
engineers might have their say. And, once having been a ship's
cook, on Christmas Captain Mulzac would himself make the
plum pudding for all his complement. Small wonder that its
mixed crew developed an *esprit de corps* second to none, and
that the *Booker T. Washington* won the honor of being one
of the cleanest and best disciplined ships in the American
Merchant Marine.

For two years one of the members of the crew of Captain Mulzac's ship was the writer, John Beecher, great-grand-
nephew of Harriet Beecher Stowe, author of "Uncle Tom's
Cabin." Beecher wrote a fascinating book called "All Brave
Sailors," subtitled, "The Story of the *S.S. Booker T. Washington*." In it are pen portraits of the men of various nationalities making up the crew, and a warm and human word pic-
ture of their skipper, Mulzac, in his paint-smeared cap, never

putting on airs of flaunting his authority, but nevertheless possessing the respect of all who came in contact with him. One of Beecher's chapters is called "Nazi Cargo" and concerns a group of five hundred German prisoners of war being transported to America on Mulzac's ship. Amusingly he writes about the astonishment of these "super-Nordics," filled as they were with contempt for Negroes, when they learn that the ship on which they are crossing to the United States is commanded by a colored man! And movingly Beecher reports the comment of one of the Germans as that voyage of the *Booker T. Washington* neared its end: "Our leaders told us that democracy in America was a fraud. They told us you were hypocritical when you said that all men were free and equal. They told us that Negroes were no better than slaves in your country. But what we have seen on this ship, the happiness, the comradeship among all of you, your fairness to us when we had been told you would beat and abuse us, all that has made us think. At night, after the lights go out down in the hold, we talk about it."

Henry Johnson
1897-1929

Henry Johnson

A GALLANT SOLDIER

 1897-1929

Of the 50,000 Negro soldiers who fought in the American armed forces during World War I, probably the most famous was Henry Johnson, a little Red Cap from Albany, New York, who became overnight a hero. In the United States some 400,000 Negroes were inducted into military service during the First World War. Of these about three-fourths were assigned to labor battalions, loading or unloading ships, salvaging war materials, detonating explosives, and burying the dead. Shortly after America's declaration of war in 1917, the first Negro stevedore battalion arrived in France. For the duration of the conflict colored soldiers on European docks handled an average of 25,000 tons of cargo a day, and were of vital importance in getting supplies to the various battle fronts. These Negro soldier-workers constituted more than one-third of the American forces on the Continent. But it was Henry Johnson's good fortune to belong to a combat unit, not a labor battalion. He was a member of the 15th National Guard of New York which became the 369th Infantry. This outfit developed into one of the foremost fighting forces in the American army. Also, it possessed the finest group of musicians in the army. The 369th Regiment Band conducted by James Reese Europe, assisted by Noble Sissle, is credited with introducing American jazz abroad. It gave concerts for all the fighting units, as well as for civilians in Paris and other cities. Of this band the soldiers often said, "They certainly have enough jazz in stock to last until the war is over."

The 369th Infantry was the first group of Negro combat troops to arrive in Europe, landing in December, 1917. That spring they withstood the Germans at Bois d'Hauza for more than two months. After a summer of training in open warfare, the outfit then went into action at Champagne, and did not cease fighting until they had reached the Rhine—the first Americans to cut through the German lines to that river. For more than six months they were continually under battle conditions. They held one trench ninety-one days without relief. They never retreated, and never was one of their men captured by the enemy. Of these fighters, their commander, Colonel William Hayward, said, "There is no better soldier material in the world." Upon the arrival of the 369th at the Rhine, the entire regiment was awarded the Croix de Guerre by the French government, having previously been cited for bravery eleven times. And two of its members, Needham Roberts and Henry Johnson, had been the first American soldiers in the war to receive individually the Croix de Guerre, awarded for unusual bravery in action.

One dark night these two privates were doing guard duty alone at an outpost not far from the enemy lines. About 2 a.m. a raiding party of some twenty Germans crept through the blackness and attacked their post with a volley of hand grenades. Both Johnson and Roberts were wounded. Roberts was hurt so badly he could not rise, but nevertheless, he was able to hand up grenades for Johnson to throw at the Germans, who by now had almost reached the post. Soon a full-scale battle was in progress between the two Negroes and the Germans. As Johnson later reported the action in conversation, he began modestly, "There isn't so much to tell. There wasn't anything so fine about it. Just fought for my life. A rabbit would have done that."

"Well, anyway, me and Needham Roberts were on patrol duty on May 15th. The corporal wanted to send out two new drafted men on the sentry post for the midnight-to-four job. I told him he was crazy to send untrained men out there and risk the rest of us. I said I'd tackle the job, though I needed sleep. German snipers had been shooting our way that night and I told the corporal he wanted men on the job who knew their rifles. He said it was imagination, but anyway he took those green men off and left Needham and me on the posts. I went on at midnight. Roberts was at the next post. At one o'clock a sniper took a crack at me from a bush fifty yards away. Pretty soon there was more firing and when Sgt. Roy Thompson came along I told him."

"What's the matter, men, you scared?" he asked.

"No, I ain't scared," I said, "I came over here to do my bit and I'll do it. But I was just lettin' you know there's liable to be some tall scrappin' around this post tonight."

"He laughed and went on, and I began to get ready. They'd a box of hand grenades there and I took them out of the box and laid them all in a row where they would be handy. There was about thirty grenades, I guess. I was goin' to bust that Dutch army in pieces if it bothered me."

"Somewhere around two o'clock I heard the Germans cutting our wire out in front and I called to Roberts. When he came I told him to pass the word to the lieutenant. He had just started off when the snippin' and clippin' of the wires sounded near, so I let go with a hand grenade. There was a yell from a lot of surprised Dutchmen and then they started firing. I hollered to Needham to come back. A German grenade got Needham in the arm and through the hip. He was too badly wounded to do any fighting, so I told him to lie in the trench and hand me up the grenades. Keep your nerve I told him. All the Dutchmen in the woods are at us, but keep cool and we'll lick 'em. Roberts crawled into the dugout, some of the shots got me, one clipped my head, another my lip, another my hand, some in my side, and one smashed my left foot."

"The Germans came from all sides. Roberts kept handing me the grenades and I kept throwing them and the Dutchmen kept squealing, but jes' the same they kept comin' on. When the grenades were all gone I started in with my rifle. That was all right until I shoved in an American cartridge clip—it was a French gun—and it jammed. There was nothing to do but use my rifle as a club and jump into them. I banged them on the dome, and the sides, and everywhere I could land until the butt of my rifle busted. One of the Germans hollered, 'Rush him! Rush him!' I decided to do some rushing myself. I grabbed my French bolo knife and slashed in a million directions. Each slash meant something, believe me. I wasn't doing exercise, let me tell you!"

By now other Germans had seized the wounded Needham Roberts and were dragging him off as a prisoner. Johnson ran after them, leaped on one of the men's shoulders, and stabbed him with a bolo knife he carried in his cartridge belt. "I picked out an officer, a lieutenant I guess he was. I got him and I got some more of them. They knocked me around considerable and whanged me on the head, but I always managed to get back on my feet. There was one guy that bothered me. He climbed on my back and I had some job shaking him off and pitching him over my head. Then I stuck him in the ribs with the bolo. I stuck one guy in the stomach and he yelled in good New York talk: 'That black so-and-so got me.' "

The Germans, as they saw one man after another fall, thought surely there must be a large number of American soldiers against them, so they turned to flee. As they scrambled through the barbed wire barricades, Johnson pelted them with hand grenades and brought down several more in pools of blood.

When this short pre-dawn encounter was over, four Germans lay dead and several more were wounded. The raiding party had abandoned seven wire cutters, three Luegers, and forty hand grenades. Johnson had rescued his badly wounded companion, Roberts, too—thus sustaining the record of the 369th that not a single man of the regiment was ever captured. Reports of this encounter of May 15, 1918, between the two Negro Americans and some twenty Germans, with the Americans routing the enemy, received wide coverage in the press. The two men were hailed as heroes, particularly Johnson who had kept his comrade in arms from being dragged away to a German prison camp. The *New York "World"* called the affray, the "Battle of Henry Johnson" and it became front page news in the American papers.

Henry Johnson, while he spent many weeks in a French hospital behind the lines, was promoted to the rank of sergeant. Most of the bones had to be removed from a shattered foot. In place of a shin bone in one leg, when he was released from the hospital, he had a silver tube. And on his body there were a half dozen permanent scars from less serious wounds. To him and to Roberts the Republic of France gave one of its proudest emblems, the Croix de Guerre with a star and golden palm. Of Roberts the citation said, "A good and brave soldier." And of Johnson, "a magnificent example of courage and energy." At war's end the French government gave to Johnson's regiment, the 369th, the signal honor of being the first Allied unit to march onto enemy soil. On November 17th, 1918, as the advance guard of the French Army of Occupation on the Rhine, the 369th took over three German towns. As one of its citations stated, this regiment had "fought with great bravery, stormed powerful enemy positions energetically defended, captured many machine guns, large numbers of prisoners, and six cannon." And among the bravest of its fighters was little Henry Johnson, a gallant soldier.

Dorie Miller

1919-1943

Dorie Miller

A HERO OF PEARL HARBOR

❧ 1919-1943 ❧

A HERO, says the dictionary, is "a doer of great or brave deeds; a man of distinguished valor or intrepidity; a prominent or central personage in any remarkable action or event." In the very first few moments of conflict at Pearl Harbor, Dorie Miller became a hero—the first Negro hero of World War II.

The twenty-three-year-old Miller was a messman on the battleship *West Virginia*—the only rating he was permitted to hold as a colored man. Before Pearl Harbor Negroes could not serve in any branch of the Navy except the stewards department; in other words, they could serve only as servants. Dorie Miller was not supposed to fire a gun. But that is just what he did on that fateful morning when the Japanese planes attacked the Pacific fleet at Pearl Harbor. While firing, he brought down four Japanese bombers.

Dorie Miller was born on a farm near Waco, Texas, the son of sharecroppers. He grew to be a big 200-pounder and the star fullback on the Moore High School football team in Waco as well as a very good boxer later. When he was nineteen Dorie enlisted in the Navy. He was nearing the end of his first stretch when the Japanese, without a declaration of

183

war, attacked the United States Naval Base in Hawaii. Early on that peaceful Sunday morning of December 7, 1941, Dorie Miller was on breakfast duty below decks, serving as a mess attendant in the junior officers' wardroom of the *West Virginia*. The night before, at various naval officers' clubs there had been the usual Saturday night dances. Many officers who had been out late had not awakened as yet so were off duty. There was little to do that morning in the almost empty mess hall. Only two men were eating. The room was quiet when suddenly Dorie heard a distant explosion. But he was accustomed to such sounds and paid no attention to it. None of the men in the mess hall knew that Japanese pilots had just dropped a bomb on the seaplane hangars at the tip of Ford Island or that the following explosion was a torpedo landing on the battleship *Utah* across the island. No one dreamed that Pearl Harbor would be attacked that Sunday morning just when the entire Pacific Fleet happened to be at anchor there. The Japanese had planned their sneak attack very carefully indeed. Four hundred of the planes swept in from the sea without interference by American aviation. Our great naval base was caught completely off-guard. For the first few moments no one knew what was happening. But within five minutes, Pearl Harbor was a shambles.

Suddenly aboard the *West Virginia* the public address system began broadcasting the alarm: "Air Raid! Air Raid! This is not a drill." In the room where Dorie Miller was waiting table, officers and messmen dropped whatever they had in hand as alarm bells rang and headed for the deck. By now the Sunday morning calm was shattered by ear-splitting detonations across the island and at that very moment a half-dozen Japanese torpedo planes were aiming at Battleship Row on the other side where, with eight more vessels, the *West Virginia* lay at anchor. A torpedo fell nearby and bullets from a straffing plane spattered the ship's deck. Then the *Oklahoma*, a few hundred yards away, was ripped by a torpedo. Two torpedoes fell on the nearby *Arizona*; then, suddenly, the *West Virginia* began to shudder from stem to stern as the first series of bombs hit her decks. Men were knocked down on their way up from quarters, others were hurled through space, lockers and tables overturned and heavy steel doors blown shut. The ship buckled and rolled beneath the impact of explosives hurtling from the skies. Just north of the *West Virginia*, the *Arizona*, squarely hit, burst into flames and exploded with an ear-splitting roar. Eleven hundred men went to their deaths aboard the ship or were blown into a harbor aflame with burning oil.

Meanwhile, Messman Dorie Miller reached the main deck of his ship just as a bomb tore away a part of the bridge and a slug of searing metal ripped into the Captain's stomach. Captain Mervyn Bennion fell to the deck, but still conscious and much concerned about what was happening to his ship. Miller lifted his captain up and carried him to a safer spot where he died. An ensign called to Miller to come and help pass ammunition to two machine gunners on the forward deck. But by then Japanese torpedoes were falling thick and fast. Bombs bursting, ammunition from the supply stacks of burning American ships flying through the air as it exploded and anti-aircraft shells falling caused general bedlam everywhere. The noise was deafening. One of the gunners Miller was asked to aid had been struck down. But the young messman who was not supposed to know how to use a machine gun took over. Dorie Miller is credited with bringing down four Japanese dive bombers before his gun was rendered useless. Amazingly enough, Dorie himself was not wounded, in spite of the straffing of enemy tailguns in the swift little planes that followed the bombers.

When the smoke of that initial battle cleared and all America knew that we were at war with the Japanese, Dorie Miller went back to being a messman again. He served aboard the aircraft carrier *Liscome Bay* where he was given an advancement to Mess Attendant Third Class. Secretary of the Navy Frank Knox had personally commended Miller for his bravery at the moment of attack. And Admiral Chester W. Nimitz, Commander-in-Chief of the Pacific Fleet, presided at the ceremonies aboard ship when Dorie Miller was awarded the Navy Cross. The Admiral personally pinned the ribbon of this medallion on the chest of the tall, dark hero, citing him for "distinguished devotion to duty, extraordinary courage and disregard for his own personal safety during the attack on Pearl Harbor."

In December 1943, Dorie Miller was killed in action in the South Pacific. Now, every year in Chicago, the Dorie Miller Memorial Foundation holds a service in his honor and in New York City a group of cooperative houses bears his name.

Benjamin O. Davis, Jr.
1912-

Benjamin O. Davis, Jr.

GENERAL OF THE AIR FORCE

∾ 1912- ∾

Upon his completion of fifty years' service in the United States Army, Brigadier General Benjamin O. Davis, Sr. received a scroll from the Commander in Chief of the Armed Forces, President Franklin D. Roosevelt. General Davis was an army career man, devoting his life to the service. His son, Benjamin O. Davis, Jr., followed in his father's footsteps and, like his father, eventually became a Brigadier General. But the elder Davis worked himself up from the ranks; the younger Davis began at West Point.

Both Davises were born in Washington, the father in 1877, the son in 1912. Benjamin Oliver Davis, Sr. attended Howard University at the capital. When the Spanish-American War broke out, Davis enlisted and saw service in Cuba. He had attained the rank of First Lieutenant when he was mustered out. And by then the army was in his blood. After three months of civilian life, he enlisted again, starting over as a buck private in a cavalry unit, but he was soon promoted to Sergeant. After five years of service he became a First Lieutenant; in 1915 a Captain; in 1917 a Major; and during World War I, a Lieutenant Colonel of the Ninth Cavalry, and one of the four top ranking Negro officers in the armed services.

In 1930 he became a full Colonel, and in 1940 a Brigadier General, the highest rank yet attained by a man of color in the United States Army.

During his long military career the elder Davis saw service in three wars as well as serving in periods of peace in the Philippine Islands, as Military Attaché to the American Legation at Monrovia, Liberia, and instructor in the science of soldiering at Wilberforce University in Ohio, at Alabama's famed Tuskegee Institute, and as commanding officer of the 369th Infantry of the New York National Guard. Among other duties in 1929 Davis escorted a large group of Gold Star mothers to Europe to visit the graves of their sons killed in World War I. During World War II he was appointed special advisor to the commander of the European Theatre of Operations. At the close of the war he became an assistant to the Inspector General of the Army, and later an advisor of the Secretary of War. In 1948 Brigadier General Davis was retired from active duty. His medals by then included the Bronze Star, the French Croix de Guerre, and the Distinguished Service Medal.

About the time that his son, Benjamin, was born, the elder Davis was recalled from Liberia and assigned to service in the Mexican Border Patrol. When Ben, Jr. was five years old, his mother died, so for a time he lived with a grandmother. But when he was about seven, his father married again, then young Ben went to live with him and his new mother at Tuskegee. Later the family moved to Cleveland, Ohio. Here Ben finished the grammar grades and was graduated as president of his class at Central High School. For a year he attended Western Reserve University, but transferred to the University of Chicago for the remainder of his college work. He majored in mathematics.

In Chicago the Negro Congressman, Oscar De Priest, took an interest in young Davis and, feeling that he should follow in his father's footsteps, appointed him a candidate for the United States Military Academy at West Point. Young Ben, however, was not sure he wanted to attend West Point, from which no Negro had been graduated in almost fifty years, since Charles Young's graduation. A number of Negroes had been appointed, but rumor had it that prejudice made life so difficult for them at the Academy that they either dropped out or had been flunked out before finishing their studies. And then, if one did graduate, there was in the United States only a strictly segregated army in which Negroes might enroll. All his life Ben's father had seen service only in all-Negro units, and in such units there was room for but a very few colored officers. Young Ben Davis did not approach his examinations for West Point with enthusiasm. And when he took them, he failed.

Perhaps it was the jolt of failure that made Ben decide to defeat his own pessimism, and to prove to himself that he *could* enter West Point—*and remain there*. Reappointed a second time, Ben settled down to several weeks of hard study. He took the examinations again, and this time passed. On the first day of July, 1932, he entered West Point. The news made all the papers, and white Americans and black Americans alike wondered if this young Negro would stick it out. He would be the only colored student at the Point and, like all freshmen, subjected to hazing on the part of upper classmen. But for him, a colored boy, would the hazing be so severe it would cause him to drop out? Would the prejudice of those who still thought of Negroes as an inferior race make life so miserable he could not stay? In his book, "We Have To-morrow," Arna Bontemps has written about Ben's experiences at West Point as follows: "There is no longer any doubt that a significant American drama was acted out during those four tense years—a drama which came close to tragedy at times and which finally had a happy ending only through the heroism of its leading character. Ben started life at West Point in the same way as any boy who has grown up in the cosmopolitan schools of great northern cities like Cleveland and Chicago. Many of the boys of his class were from the same general background. They were like the fellows at the University and at Central High. Ben made acquaintances among them swiftly and seemed on the way to a normal school year, when something happened. It started with whispers in locker rooms and in hallways. Somebody was passing a word around. Ben could feel rather than hear what they were saying, and he was sure that the 'word' concerned him. Within a day or two he knew it, for all the boys stopped speaking to him. Somebody had organized the demonstration and the others, boy-like and easily led, took it up and fell in line. Few could have realized the unfairness, the unworthiness of this behavior. Perhaps some of the boys resisted those who took the lead, but feared to stand out against what they believed to be the majority. In any case, it continued and became more marked as time passed. Nobody did anything which could be described as hostile of itself, yet nobody co-operated with Ben. No one greeted him. If he asked a simple question he was not answered. If he approached a group in which a conversation was in progress, all talking suddenly ceased. He was left alone —completely alone. His classmates were giving him the 'silent treatment.' . . . It is hard to believe that any group of boys could continue a demonstration of this kind for a whole year. It is also hard to believe that a solitary colored boy could last it out—especially when one remembers how easy it is to give up under a strain. The silence, with slight interruptions, lasted through Ben's plebe year, and Ben stood up to it until the end. Taller than most of his fellows, as handsome as anybody who wore the uniform, as fond of companionship and good fun as any boy, Ben took what was dished out to him without a whimper or a complaint. Never once did he let anyone think that he depended on others for his happiness. He simply took the medicine.

"The demonstration ended even more dramatically than it had begun. At the end of the first year at the Military Academy there is always an important gathering at which those plebes who have stood up under the hard conditioning of the testing year are congratulated by their superiors and in turn congratulate each other. Ben Davis came to this annual ceremony congratulating himself silently and thinking that at least he had accomplished something for all those colored people who had kept their fingers crossed as they waited to see what would happen to this second colored boy to face the grim music of West Point in recent years. . . . To his complete surprise, however, a miracle happened. When the preliminaries were over and the boys were free to congratulate each other and to receive the congratulations of upperclassmen, Ben suddenly discovered that he was surrounded. They swarmed around him. They cheered him noisily and shook his hand until his arm was weak. Ben Davis, Jr. had stood the most severe test any boy had stood at West Point in at least fifty years, and he had passed it to the satisfaction of the whole class of his fellows. The wall of silence fell down like the walls of Jericho, and was never raised again."

On June 12, 1936, the graduation ceremonies were held and Benjamin O. Davis, Jr. received his diploma from General John J. Pershing, plus his commission as Second Lieutenant.

That same year he married Agatha Scott of New Haven, and was assigned as an officer of infantry at Fort Benning, Georgia, in the heart of the South. A year later he was promoted to First Lieutenant; in 1939 he became a Captain, then a Major, and in 1942 a Lieutenant Colonel. Meanwhile he had served as a Professor of Military Tactics at Tuskegee, and as Aide-de-Camp to his father during his time as Commanding General of the 4th Cavalry Brigade at Fort Riley, Kansas. While young Davis was at Fort Riley in 1940 the Air Force, which had hitherto not admitted Negroes as pilots, changed its policy, and established an Advanced Army Flying School for the training of young colored officers at Tuskegee. Davis was among the first to enroll in the spring of 1941, and the following year he won his wings. Meanwhile, the United States had become embroiled in World War II. Upon graduation from the Army Flying School, Davis was placed in command of the all-Negro 99th Pursuit Squadron then preparing to go overseas to the European battlefronts. The members of this Squadron were the first group of colored pilots to undergo combat service in the American military forces, and their record as bomber escorts and on perilous strafing missions became a gallant one.

So successful was the leadership of young Colonel Davis that in the fall of 1943 he was recalled to the States to direct the training of the 332nd Fighter Group then in formation at Selfridge Field, Michigan. Under his command, the 332nd was assigned to the Mediterranean Theatre as a part of the 12th Fighter Command. This oufit participated in the sinking of an enemy destroyer, protected the 15th Air Force Bombers in their strategic attacks on the Rumanian oil fields, and in the North African and Italian campaigns brought down more than a hundred planes in the air and knocked out a hundred and fifty on the ground. Most of the pilots of the 332nd received the Distinguished Flying Cross.

When the Allied invasion of southern France was planned, to the 332nd Fighter Group under Colonel Davis was given the vital task of destroying the German radar stations on the Mediterranean coast in advance of the Allied landings. The night before the invasion the Negro flyers went into action. They did so thorough a job of knocking out the various enemy bases for air-protection and communications, that when the surprise attack came, the Germans were caught completely off-guard, so among Allied troops there was a minimum of casualties. From destroyers off shore, Prime Minister Winston Churchill and other Allied leaders watched the progress of the highly successful attack, and had only praise for the colored aviators who had prepared the way so well. Many of these men were awarded medals. And Brigadier General Benjamin O. Davis, Sr. proudly pinned on the chest of his son, Colonel Benjamin O. Davis, Jr., the Distinguished Flying Cross. Members of the 332nd participated in the ceremonies. By war's end this intrepid group had flown over Europe more than 3,000 missions and had put out of action some three hundred enemy planes.

As fighters for the Free World, the colored aviators who served under Colonel Davis were also fighting for a greater share of democracy for themselves and their race, not only in the armed forces, but in civilian life on the home front. As to the American military set-up—then undergoing a transition from separate, segregated units of either all-white or all-Negro groups—the contributions which the heroism and daring of these colored aviators made to the cause of interracial good will was invaluable. In 1944 the Negro journalist Roi Ottley, reporting from the battlefronts, wrote:

"I have heard more than one Southerner say he hoped, when the war is over, that Negroes would enjoy the social benefits that they are fighting to preserve and extend. The Air Force has perhaps achieved the greatest amount of mutual respect and admiration among its personnel. Negro aviators have been overseas in combat more than nineteen months. They have seen action from Munich to Vienna, from Salerno to Budapest, and from North Africa to Sicily. They have won commendation from General Montgomery for their dive-bombing and strafing of enemy positions both in the Italian and North African campaigns. In the desperate Anzio beachhead assaults, they shot down seventeen enemy fighters and bombers in one day, providing cover for our ground forces. This sort of performance is difficult to refute with nonsense about the 'inferiority' of the Negro, for the facts stand out dramatically and must of necessity make deep inroads into the thinking of every white G.I."

That same year, in addressing the 23rd class of Negro pilots to be graduated from the Tuskegee Army Air Field, their white commanding officer, Colonel Noel Parrish, recalled the exploits of that field's early Negro graduates flying so brilliantly under Colonel Davis. In concluding his speech, he said in part:

"Today the problems of race are still somewhat bewildering. Perhaps we can all find truth earlier if we will take the attitude of mutual respect and understanding, and remember that in all things white people are just as much the victims of their environment and training, or lack of training, as are Negroes. . . . To you the problem of racial adjustment is constant and inescapable. You cannot run away. . . . You must continue to hold up your heads against pity and hatred alike, to do your best and hope for the best. Such advice is easier to give than to follow, but I know of no other way. It is the way you learned to fly. Few of us choose to fight against odds, but perhaps there is some compensation in the fact that to win against them brings a greater glory and a greater personal satisfaction. . . . You will have many disillusionments and embarrassments and perhaps some bewilderment as to just what is desired or expected of you. But men who have the patience and the perseverance to win through the rugged training program you have just finished must have the stamina and courage to achieve even greater things in the future. You now have before you the example of others who have proved it can be done. You can play a mighty part in the greatest battle for all freedom, including your own. See that you are worthy of those who have gone out from this field ahead of you and that you provide an even more inspiring example for those who follow."

The men who had left Tuskegee Air Field before, in 1944 were still in the thick of warfare, and they finished out the conflict with distinction. At the conclusion of hostilities their leader, Colonel Davis, was assigned to the Lockbourne Air Base as commander of the 477th Composite Fighter-Bomber Group. There had been considerable opposition on the part of whites to the stationing of Negro flyers at this major base, but the War Department paid it no heed. Negroes were now being trained as navigators, bombardiers, flight engineers, and in air corps administration, and integration of personnel at various fields was proceeding apace. Colonel Davis remained at Lockbourne until he was assigned for study at the Air War College at Maxwell Base, Montgomery, Alabama from which he was graduated in 1950. After a period of administrative service at the Air Force Headquarters in Washington, he was appointed by President Eisenhower in 1954 as director of operations and training of the Far Eastern Air Forces in Japan, and in 1955 he was made 2nd in command, and later commander of the 13th Air Task Force on the Chinese Nationalist island of Formosa, having by now been raised to the rank of Brigadier General. Early in 1957 Davis was appointed a member of the Air Force Board at the Pentagon, and later that year named Deputy Chief of Staff of the 12th Air Force in Germany.

This important assignment made General Davis the third highest ranking officer in the German area of command.

Stationed at Ramstein, his work became that of coordinator of the various units of the 12th Air Force, a vital group in the NATO defense plans for Western Europe. From a pessimistic young man who flunked his first examinations for West Point to a flying hero of World War II and now a most valuable officer of the Air Force, Benjamin O. Davis, Jr. well deserves to wear the medals that have been bestowed upon him. Aside from the Distinguished Flying Cross, some are the Air Medal with four Oak Leaf Clusters, the Legion of Merit Award, and the French Croix de Guerre with Palm. For conducting successfully an extremely hazardous mission over Berlin, Davis and his entire 332nd Fighter Group received a Presidential citation—which made his father, a fifty-year veteran, very proud. The two Davises have served their country, militarily speaking, for a long time. And they have served it well.

Index

Index

INDEX

LANGSTON HUGHES

often termed the Poet Laureate of the Negro people, was born in Joplin, Missouri, in 1902, and his literary career began as Class Poet in the eighth grade. He attended Central High School in Cleveland, Ohio, and received an A.B. degree in 1929 from Lincoln University in Pennsylvania, by which he was subsequently awarded an Honorary Lit.D. degree in 1943.

Hughes' first book of poems, *The Weary Blues*, was published in 1925. That same year, he won national attention when Vachel Lindsay read three of his poems on a program at the Wardman Park Hotel, in Washington, D.C., where Hughes was employed as a busboy. Since that time he has written a dozen books, in addition to many stories, poems and articles for leading magazines. His work includes opera librettoes and Broadway shows as well as material for radio and motion pictures.

In 1927, he received the Palms Intercollegiate Poetry Award and two years later the Harmon Gold Award for Literature for his novel *Not Without Laughter*. Holder of a Guggenheim Fellowship in 1935 and a Rosenwald Fellowship five years later, Hughes received in 1946 an honorary grant from the American Academy of Arts and Letters.

He is the author of a weekly column in the *Chicago Defender* and has lectured and read his poems throughout the United States and abroad. Langston Hughes' works are concerned mainly with Negro life in America, and among his recent books are *Simple Stakes a Claim* and the *First Book of the West Indies*. His play with music, *Simply Heavenly*, has been produced in New York, Hollywood and London.